Diet recommendations in case of malignant diseases

Please check these recommendations always with a nutrition consultant, therapist, doctor or dietician. The recipes and the list of ingredients are supporting the conventional medical therapy.
The calorie disclosures of fresh ingredients (fruit and vegetables) vary according to quality and time of harvest. The contents were checked by a dietician and a nutrition consultant for the Traditional Chinese Medicine (TCM).

Author:
©2017 Josef Miligui
www.ebns.at

AF285343

Source:
The lists are created from the EBNS database for nutritional counseling. The database is used by dietitians, therapists and doctors for advising the patient / client.

Literature:
The specialist literature and the training documents of the German and Austrian dietary and traditional Chinese medicine serve as a knowledge base. We have used the documents as a basis of knowledge, adapted it to our experience and completed them.
http://di-book.com

Title Photo:
©2008 Erika Weixlbaumer

Production and publishing:
BoD – Books on Demand, Norderstedt
ISBN: 9783752829327

Diet recommendations for DIETETICS - Changed nutrient requirements - in case of malignant diseases

1   Treatment strategy

Have a therapist perform a nutritional history to take into account previous eating habits, nutrient supply, preferences for certain foods and drinks, aversions, intolerances, disturbances of taste, or swallowing problems.

Demand-adjusted increase in food supply.

Protein 1.3-2 g per kg normal weight.

Fat 1.5-2 g per kg normal weight.

Carbohydrates 4-7 g per kg normal weight.

Calories 35-40 kcal per kg normal weight.

Vitamin substitution after consultation with the treating physician.

2   Avoid

Smoking, coffee, sugar, alcohol, spicy food. raw meat and sausage products, smoked food, stress.

3 Breakfast

4 Snack

5 Lunch

6 Afternoon

7 Dinner

8   Any time

9 Recipes

(recommendable) = You can use more.
(little) = You should use less than specified or omit.

9.1 Andalusian fish pot

Strengthens immune system, prevents cancer, dissolves stagnation, promotes weight loss. Good to fight immunodeficiency, loss of appetite, flatulence, high blood pressure, depressions, diabetes, diarrhea, stimulates appetite.
Cooking time approx. 30 min
Calories p. portion: 348
4 portions
Allergens: ADLO

Quantity of ingredients:
Basic recipe for a vegetable soup (nutritious) 2 cups / 500g. (yes)
Onion (spring onion) 2 pieces / 40g. (yes)
Olive oil 1 table spoon / 20g. (yes)
Lemon peel 1/2 piece / 3g. (yes)
Bay leaf 1 piece / 1g. (yes)
Potato 5/8 oz / 200g. (yes)
Cod 3/4 lbs / 300g. (yes)
White wine 4 table spoons / 80g. (little)
Lemon juice 1/2 teaspoon / 10g. (yes)
Salt 1 pinch / 1g. (little)
Pepper (ground) 1 pinch / 0,2g. (yes)
Parsley 1 table spoon / 15g. (yes)
White bread (wheat bread) 8 slices / 250g. (yes)

Cooking instructions:
Boil the vegetable broth with small spring onion, olive oil, grated lemon peel and bay leaf. Boil covered for 10 minutes. Add the peeled, diced potatoes and boil in about 8 minutes. Add fish pieces and white wine and switch to small heat. In the slightly boiling broth put the fish and boil it a few minutes. Season with lemon juice, salt and pepper. Serve with parsley sprinkled.
White bread as a side dish.

9.2 Asparagus and herb ragout

Diuretic, improves blood circulation, prevents cancer, dissolves stagnation, promotes weight loss. Good to fight immunodeficiency, loss of appetite, flatulence, high blood pressure, depressions, diabetes, diarrhea, stimulates liver function.
Cooking time approx. 30 min
Calories p. portion: 168
4 portions
Allergens: GL

Quantity of ingredients:
Basic recipe for a vegetable soup (nutritious) 2 cups / 500g. (yes)
Lemon peel 1/2 piece / 3g. (yes)
Coriander 1/4 teaspoon / 1g. (yes)
Nutmeg 1 pinch / 0,3g. (yes)
Asparagus (green or white) 1,8 lbs / 800g. (yes)
Parsley 1 Bunch / 125g. (yes)
Créme fraiche cheese 2 table spoons / 30g. (yes)
Lemon juice 1 teaspoon / 3g. (yes)
Potato 7/8 lbs / 400g. (yes)

Cooking instructions:
Cook potatoes with plenty of salted water about 20 min. until soft.
Heat the vegetable stock with lemon zest, coriander and nutmeg till it boil. Cook the peeled and sliced asparagus in it.
Drain asparagus in a sieve. Collect the cooking liquid.
In the blender mix 200 g of cooked asparagus (the lower ends), cooking liquid and parsley to a smooth sauce. Beat the sauce with crème fraiche until smooth. Add asparagus and heat again and season with lemon juice, salt and pepper. Serve with the potatoes.

9.3 Asparagus Cream Soup

Diuretic, improves blood circulation, prevents cancer, laxative, antiparasitic, stimulates liver function, good to fight loss of appetite, flatulence, rheumatism, heartburn.
Cooking time approx. 45 min
Calories p. portion: 240
2 portions
Allergens: ACG

Quantity of ingredients:
Asparagus (green or white) 5/8 oz / 200g. (yes)
Water 2 cup / 500g. (yes)
Rapeseed oil 2 table spoons / 30g. (yes)
Wheat flour 2 table spoons / 10g. (yes)
Chicken yolk 1 piece / 25g. (yes)
Cow's milk (whole milk 3.5% fat) 1 table spoon / 15g. (recommended)
Sour cream 15% fat 1 table spoon / 15g. (recommended)
Pepper (ground) 1 pinch / 0,5g. (yes)
Nutmeg 1 pinch / 0,5g. (yes)
Lemon juice 1 teaspoon / 2g. (yes)
Parsley 2 table spoons / 20g. (yes)
Salt 1 pinch / 1g. (little)

Cooking instructions:
Wash and peel the asparagus.
Heat water, a little lemon juice and pinch of salt till it boils. Tie the asparagus spears together.
Add the asparagus peel to the cooking water and bring to the boil.
Add the asparagus and cook on low heat for about 20 minutes.
Then remove the asparagus bunches and pour the broth through a sieve.
For the roux, heat the oil in a saucepan, add the flour and sauté until it is colorless, slowly top up with the asparagus sauce and simmer for 10 minutes. Cut the asparagus spears into pieces about 3 cm long and place them to the soup.

Just before serving, bring the soup to the boil again.
Mix the egg yolk with the milk and sour cream.
Remove the pot from the heat and stir in the egg yolk and milk mixture.
Season with pepper and nutmeg, decorate with the chopped parsley and serve immediately.

9.4   Asparagus with lemon pesto

Diuretic, improves blood circulation, prevents cancer, forcing spleen, promotes weight loss. Good to fight immunodeficiency, loss of appetite, arteriosclerosis, flatulence, bladder weakness, anemia, high blood pressure, depressions, diabetes, diarrhea, vomiting.
Cooking time approx. 20 min
Calories p. portion: 172
2 portions
Allergens: H

Quantity of ingredients:
Asparagus (green or white) 1,1 lbs / 500g. (yes)
Lemon 1 piece / 35g. (yes)
Water hot 1/2 cup / 50g. (yes)
Boxhorn clover seeds 1 pinch / 0,2g. (yes)
Olive oil 2 table spoons / 20g. (yes)
Almond 1 table spoon / 8g. (yes)
Sugar cane sugar 1 pinch / 0,5g. (recommended)
Garlic 1 clove / 2g. (yes)
Pepper (ground) 1 pinch / 0,2g. (yes)
Salt 1 pinch / 0,5g. (little)

Cooking instructions:
Peel the asparagus (the whites whole, the greens only at the bottom). Peel and cut diagonally into pieces about 3 cm long. In the steam sieve the white about 12 minutes, the green about 10 minutes to cook. Cut the lemon into small pieces, remove seeds. Add the remaining ingredients and puree to a creamy sauce. Arrange the asparagus and cover with the lemon pesto.
This fits rice, bulgur or millet.

9.5 Basic recipe for a chicken broth worming

Strengthens blood, strengthens bone marrow, reduces blood pressure, strengthens immune system, prevents cancer, reduces radiation damage, promotes sweating, dissolves stagnation, good to fight loss of appetite, flatulence.
Cooking time approx. 2-3 hours
Calories p. portion: 90
9 portions
Allergens: L

Quantity of ingredients:
Chicken meat 1/2 piece / 600g. (yes)
Carrot 2 pieces / 150g. (yes)
Leek 1 stick / 45g. (yes)
Celery root 1 piece / 500g. (yes)
Ginger fresh 2 slices / 2g. (yes)
Fenugreek (Trigonella foenum-graecum) 1 teaspoon / 2g. (yes)
Juniper berry 1 teaspoon / 3g. (yes)
Bay leaf 3 pieces / 2g. (yes)
Water 4 cup / 900g. (yes)

Cooking instructions:
Remove chicken parts from fat. Place chicken pieces in a saucepan with hot water and heat till it boils briefly, skimming any resulting foam. Add coarsely chopped vegetables and all spices and cook over medium heat for 2 to 3 hours. Strain the finished soup. Throw away vegetables and bones.
Tip: If you want to use the meat as a soup insert, take out after 45 minutes and return only the bones in the soup.
Refrigerate for later use.

9.6 Basic recipe for a fish broth

Strengthens the kidneys, promotes watering, reduces blood pressure, strengthens immune system, prevents cancer, reduces radiation damage. Low in cholesterol and protein rich. Improves blood circulation, stimulates appetite.
Cooking time approx. 40 min
Calories p. portion: 128
5 portions
Allergens: DLO

Quantity of ingredients:
Fish pieces mixed (fresh water) 3/4 lbs / 300g. (yes)
Celery root 1/4 lbs - 4oz / 120g. (yes)
Leek 2 inches / 10g. (yes)
Carrot 2 pieces / 150g. (yes)
White wine 1/2 cup / 125g. (little)
Lemon 1/2 piece / 50g. (yes)
Bay leaf 2 leaves / 2g. (yes)
Peppercorns 3 pieces / 2g. (yes)
Olive oil 1 table spoon / 10g. (yes)
Water 2 cup / 450g. (yes)

Cooking instructions:
Fry celery, chopped carrots and leeks in olive oil, add bay leaf and peppercorns, add pieces of fish and sauté briefly. Add water, add little white wine or lemon. Simmer gently for 30 minutes. Skim off the resulting foam several times. In the end, sift the ingredients through a cloth.
Refrigerate for later use

9.7 Basic recipe for a reissue soup (Congee)

Low fat content, for the drainage of the body overweight and high blood pressure.
Cooking time approx. 2-4 hours
Calories p. portion: 140
3 portions
Allergens:
Quantity of ingredients:
Rice variety any 1 cup / 120g. (yes)
Water 6 cups / 700g. (yes)

Cooking instructions:
Cook rice and water in a ratio of about 1: 6. The amount of water determines the thickness of the mash (matter of taste).
Put the rice in a saucepan with a heavy lid. It is important to simmer the rice after a short boil on the slightest flame, otherwise it burns.
Boil the rice for 2-4 hours. The longer he cooks, the more he strengthens.
If you want to eat the dish for breakfast, you can put the rice on just before bedtime.
To be on the safe side, you should first check the behavior of your pot and cooker under observation for a similar amount of time, so that nothing burns.
Refrigerate for later use.

9.8 Basic recipe for a vegetable soup, nutritious

Reduces blood pressure, strengthens immune system, prevents cancer, forcing spleen, dissolves stagnation, promotes weight loss. Good to fight immunodeficiency, high blood pressure, depressions, diabetes, diarrhea, reduces blood lipids.
Cooking time approx. 2-3 hours
Calories p. portion: 48
5 portions
Allergens: L

Quantity of ingredients:
Olive oil 1 table spoon / 4g. (yes)
Onion white 1 piece / 60g. (yes)
Carrot 3 pieces / 200g. (yes)
Parsnip 3/8 lbs - 6oz / 150g. (yes)
Celery root 1 cup / 100g. (yes)
Ginger fresh 1/2 teaspoon / 2g. (yes)

Lemon 1/2 piece / 25g. (yes)
Juniper berry 6 pieces / 6g. (yes)
Thyme dried 1 pinch / 1g. (yes)
Lovage 1 table spoon / 3g. (yes)
Bay leaf 2 leaves / 1g. (yes)
Salt 1 pinch / 1g. (little)
Water 3 cups / 650g. (yes)

Cooking instructions:
Cut the vegetables into cubes.
Heat oil in hot pot, fry shortly onions and vegetables.
Add cold water, then add ginger, bay leaf and lemon juice.
Season with juniper, thyme and lovage. Cover for 2 - 3 hours on a low heat and simmer.
The used vegetables should be thrown away.
The basic recipe serves as a soup base and to refine vegetables, legumes or cereals.
If you want to eat vegetable soup immediately, add the desired vegetables half an hour before.
Refrigerate for later use.

9.9   Basmati rice + Zucchini tofu dish

Diuretic, supports urination, harmonizes spleen and stomach, reduces flatulence, good to fight body overweight and high blood pressure. Antioxidativ, promotes digestion, perspiration, reduces blood lipids, forcing spleen.
Cooking time approx. 20 min
Calories p. portion: 146
4 portions
Allergens: E

Quantity of ingredients:
Soy Tofu 5/8 lbs - 8oz / 250g. (yes)
Olive oil 2 table spoons / 6g. (yes)
Coriander 1/2 teaspoon / 4g. (yes)
Ginger fresh 1/2 teaspoon / 4g. (yes)
Rice Basmati 1/2 cup / 60g. (yes)
Water 3 cups / 200g. (yes)
Zucchini 1 piece / 700g. (yes)

Cooking instructions:
Cut tofu cubes and marinate with olive oil, tamari, crushed coriander

and ginger. Leave at least 1 hour.

Cook Basmati rice with the water. You can season with onion and cardamom.
Roast zucchini and tofu in pan in the hot oil for approx. 5-7 min.
Serve rice and tofu on a plate.
Add the parsley.

Can also be used as a salad for the home and on the go.

9.10 Beef soup with colorful vegetables and mushrooms

Strengths spleen and stomach, strengthens blood, strengthens the muscles, tendons and bones. Diuretic, harmonizes the stomach and intestines, Conducts bowel winds. Promotes normal thyroid function. Strengthens gastrointestinal function, expands blood vessels.
Cooking time approx. 2-6 hours
Calories p. portion: 142
6 portions
Allergens: EO

Quantity of ingredients:
Water 3 cups / 700g. (yes)
Lemon 1 dash / 2g. (yes)
Pepper powder (hot) 1 pinch / 0,3g. (yes)
Beef meat 1,1 lbs / 500g. (yes)
Broccoli 1 cup cutted / 100g. (yes)
Kohlrabi 1 cup diced / 100g. (yes)
Ginger fresh 1 inch / 3g. (yes)
Oregano fresh 2 table spoons / 6g. (yes)
Soy sauce 1 dash / 1g. (yes)
White wine 2 table spoons / 20g. (little)
Oyster mushroom 4-6 pieces / 20g. (yes)
Chinese cabbage 3-4 table spoons (cut) / 30g. (yes)
Pepper (ground) 1 pinch / 0,2g. (yes)
Onion (spring onion) 2-3 pieces / 50g. (yes)
Salt 1 pinch / 0,5g. (little)

Cooking instructions:
Heat in a saucepan with water (enough to cover the meat), a dash of lemon juice, a pinch of rose paprika, beef stew or leg slice, till it boils and simmer for a moment; then pour off the broth, rinse the meat with

hot water (this will save you from foaming), clean the pot and put the meat in hot water again; chopped stalks of broccoli, chopped kohlrabi, a piece of sliced ginger; simmer until the meat is cooked; abundant dried oregano,
Add soy sauce, white wine or lemon juice, some rose paprika or fresh oregano, oyster mushrooms cut into strips or shiitake mushrooms, add the broccoli florets, chopped Chinese cabbage; simmer until the ingredients are cooked; ground pepper, add plenty of chopped green onions; simmer briefly, season with salt, lemon juice.

9.11 Beet salad with salad cucumber

Diuretic, detoxifying, suppresses conversion of sugar into fat, lowers cholesterol. Improves blood circulation, strengthens the muscles, antioxidativ. Strengthens gastrointestinal function, expands blood vessels, bactericide.
Cooking time approx. 45 min
Calories p. portion: 246
2 portions
Allergens: GMO

Quantity of ingredients:
Red beet 4 pieces / 200g. (yes)
Cucumber 1 piece / 250g. (yes)
Olive oil 4 table spoons / 40g. (yes)
Sugar cane sugar 1 pinch / 1g. (recommended)
Pepper (ground) 1 pinch / 0,2g. (yes)
Mustard seeds 1 pinch of powder / 0,2g. (yes)
Dill 1/2 teaspoon (chopped) / 2g. (yes)
Onion (spring onion) 2 pieces / 40g. (yes)
Salt 1 pinch / 0,5g. (little)
Vinegar (Apple vinegar) 1 dash / 1g. (yes)
Sour cream 15% fat 2 table spoons / g. (recommended)
Pepper powder (hot) 1 pinch / 0,3g. (yes)

Cooking instructions:
Softly boil beetroot, peel and dice; Peel and dice the cucumber.
Dressing: olive oil, a little whole cane sugar, pepper, mustard powder, dill, finely chopped spring onion, salt, vinegar, a little sour cream and a pinch of rose paprika; stir; mix with the beetroot and let it rest; Add the cucumbers just before serving to keep their light color.
Serve with: millet, which together with the salad makes a simple, light meal.

9.12 Boiled celery salad with exotic spices

Forcing spleen, relieves diarrhea, antibacterial, blood-forming, blood detoxifying, reduces inflammation, diuretic, improves blood circulation.
Cooking time approx. 30 min
Calories p. portion: 166
4 portions
Allergens: GLMNO

Quantity of ingredients:
Celery root 1 1/2 piece / 900g. (yes)
Yogurt (natural, 3.5% fat) 1 cup / 250g. (recommended)
Sour cream 15% fat 2 table spoons / 20g. (recommended)
Turmeric (yellow root) 1 pinch / 1g. (yes)
Sesame oil 1 table spoon / 20g. (yes)
Pepper (ground) 1 pinch / 0,5g. (yes)
Lemongrass 1 pinch / 1g. (yes)
Onion white 1/2 piece / 25g. (yes)
Mustard 1/2 teaspoon / 1g. (yes)
Black caraway 1 pinch / 1g. (yes)
Salt 1 pinch / 1g. (little)
Lemon juice 1 piece / 40g. (yes)
Apple (sour) 1/2 piece / 100g. (recommended)
Peppers powder 1 pinch / 1g. (yes)
Vinegar (Apple vinegar) 1 dash / 3g. (yes)

Cooking instructions:
Cook the peeled celeriac in thick slices and then cut into bite-sized strips.
Dressing: Mix a little yoghurt, sour cream, turmeric, sesame oil, pepper, lemongrass powder, finely chopped onion, a little mustard, salt, crushed black cumin, some cold water, lemon juice or vinegar; add the sour chopped apple, some rose paprika, the lukewarm celery and mix well; let it rest for 2 - 3 hours or overnight. Ideal as a substitute for raw food

9.13 Carrot and potato rucola sandwich

Reduces inflammation, improves digestion, supports urination, lowers cholesterol, strengthens immune system, prevents cancer, good to fight constipation (Fibre-rich), dissolves stagnation.
Cooking time approx. 20 min
Calories p. portion: 94
4 portions
Allergens: AG

Quantity of ingredients:
Potato (mealy) 5/8 oz / 200g. (yes)
Carrot 1 piece / 50g. (yes)
Sour cream 15% fat 2 table spoons / 45g. (recommended)
Onion (spring onion) 1 piece / 20g. (yes)
Rucola 1/2 bunch / 100g. (yes)
Lemon peel 1/4 teaspoon / 1g. (yes)
Salt 1 pinch / 1g. (little)
Pepper (ground) 1 pinch / 0,2g. (yes)
Whole grain bread 8 slices / 48g. (yes)

Cooking instructions:
Cook the potatoes gently, peel and squeeze through the potato press.
Cook vegetable broth according to the basic recipe and remove a carrot
after a short cooking time and finely crush with a fork.
Stir the potatoes, carrots, grated lemon zest and sour cream into a
smooth cream.
Mix carrot and potato cream with finely chopped rocket salad. Season
the spread with salt and pepper and spread the bread. Sprinkle with the
finely chopped young onions.

9.14 Carrot drink

Promotes spleen and liver, reduces blood pressure, strengthens
immune system, prevents cancer, reduces radiation damage, diuretic,
building up, eye-enhancing, detoxifying, nerve-strengthening.
Cooking time approx. 15 min
Calories p. portion: 143
1 portions
Allergens: H

Quantity of ingredients:
Millet flakes 1 table spoon / 10g. (yes)
Carrot 7/8 lbs / 200g. (yes)
Almond puree 1 teaspoon / 3g. (yes)
Honey 1/2 teaspoon / 2g. (recommended)
Water / 50g. (yes)

Cooking instructions:
Sprinkle millet flakes with 50 ml of cold water and let it swell for 10 minutes.
Juice the fresh carrots or use 200 ml. carrot juice.
Puree the millet flakes, carrot juice, almond paste and honey with the blender.

9.15 Carrots with potato foam

Promotes spleen and liver, reduces blood pressure, strengthens immune system. Improves digestion, regenerates skin, supports urination, lowers cholesterol, promotes the production of stool and urine, strengthens blood, strengthens nerves.
Cooking time approx. 30 min
Calories p. portion: 316
1 portions
Allergens: G

Quantity of ingredients:
Carrot (Early Carrot) 3/8 lbs - 6oz / 150g. (yes)
Pork meat 1/8 lbs - 2oz / 40g. (yes)
Potato (mealy) 1/4 lbs - 4oz / 100g. (yes)
Butter organic 1 table spoon / 10g. (yes)
Honey 1/2 teaspoon / 2g. (recommended)
Anise (Common Fennel) 1 pinch / 0,2g. (yes)
Water 2 table spoons / 20g. (yes)

Cooking instructions:
Clean the carrots, wash thoroughly, peel thinly and cut into thin slices.
Cut the meat into strips.
Wash the potatoes, cook in a small saucepan with little water in about 15 minutes.
Melt half of the butter in a saucepan, fry the carrots and the meat in it. If necessary, add 2-3 tablespoons of water, put the lid on and cook everything over low heat in about 15 minutes.
Add the honey, the anise and the remaining butter and remove the pot from the heat.
Peel the potatoes and press directly onto the plate with the potato press. Distribute the honey carrots over it.

9.16 Cod soup with tomatoes

Promotes spleen and kidney; promotes watering. Strengthens the kidneys. Improves blood circulation, improves medication effect, stimulates appetite, helps to digest fat, supports urination, reduces blood pressure, stimulates liver function, detoxifying.
Cooking time approx. 30 min
Calories p. portion: 176
4 portions
Allergens: DLO

Quantity of ingredients:
Basic recipe for a fish soup 2 cup / 450g. (yes)
Cod 5/8 lbs - 8oz / 250g. (yes)
Onion (shallot) 1 piece / 20g. (yes)
Anise (Common Fennel) 1/2 teaspoon / 1g. (yes)
Ginger fresh 1/2 teaspoon / 1g. (yes)
Olive oil 1 teaspoon / 3g. (yes)
Tomato 1 piece / 50g. (yes)
White wine 1/2 cup / 125g. (little)
Salt 1 pinch / 0,5g. (little)
Pepper (ground) 1 pinch / 0,2g. (yes)
Parsley 1 table spoon (chopped) / 5g. (yes)

Cooking instructions:
Fry the onion, anise and freshly grated ginger in oil.
Add finely chopped tomatoes and sauté. Add a little wine and fish soup. Simmer gently for 10-15 minutes. Season with salt and pepper; Add the cod pieces and heat gently. Garnish with parsley at the end.

9.17 Compote from plums

Cancer preventive effect, dehydrates the body, stimulates digestion and binds fats in the intestine.
Cooking time approx. 10 min
Calories p. portion: 22
2 portions
Allergens:
Quantity of ingredients:
Plums 1/4 lbs - 4oz / 100g. (yes)
Water 1 1/2 cups / 240g. (yes)
Cinnamon ground 1 pinch / 1g. (yes)

Cooking instructions:
Boil plums in water until soft. Sprinkle with a little cinnamon.

9.18 Couscous Salad

prevents cancer, forcing spleen, promotes digestion, stimulates liver
function, reduces blood pressure, strengthens immune system, reduces
radiation damage, diuretic.
Cooking time approx. 25 min
Calories p. portion: 338
3 portions
Allergens: A

Quantity of ingredients:
Water 1 cup / 100g. (yes)
Olive oil 1 table spoon / 15g. (yes)
Couscous 5/8 oz / 200g. (yes)
Lemon juice 2 table spoons / 30g. (yes)
Lemon peel 1 teaspoon / 2g. (yes)
Tomato 2 pieces / 80g. (yes)
Cucumber 1/4 lbs - 4oz / 100g. (yes)
Carrot 1/4 lbs - 4oz / 100g. (yes)
Parsley 1 Bunch / 100g. (yes)
Chives 1 Bunch / 100g. (yes)
Peppermint 3 twigs / 30g. (yes)

Cooking instructions:
Boil in a small saucepan 250 ml. water with salt and 1 tablespoon olive
oil. Add the couscous, take the stove in the front and let it swell covered
for 5 minutes. Put the couscous back on the stove and let it simmer for
about 2 minutes with gentle stirring. If necessary, add 1 - 3 tbsp of hot
water.
Mix the couscous with lemon juice, chopped lemon peel and 1 tbsp oil,
season with salt and pepper and leave to set.
Add couscous with tomatoes, cucumber, parsley (all diced), carrots
(grated), chives and mint (finely chopped). Season the couscous salad
with lemon juice, salt and pepper.

9.19 Cucumber salad

Diuretic, detoxifying, suppresses conversion of sugar into fat, lowers cholesterol, prevents cancer. Cucumber cools and moistens. Dill works against flatulence, anticonvulsant in gastrointestinal discomfort.
Cooking time approx. 5 min
Calories p. portion: 27
2 portions
Allergens: O

Quantity of ingredients:
Cucumber 1 piece / 400g. (yes)
Salt 1 pinch / 1g. (little)
Dill 1 pinch / 1g. (yes)
Vinegar (Apple vinegar) 1 table spoon / 10g. (yes)

Cooking instructions:
Cut the cucumber (do not peel the BIO) thinly and season.

9.20 Cucumber soup

Diuretic, detoxifying, suppresses conversion of sugar into fat, lowers cholesterol, prevents cancer, promotes digestion, diaphoretic, dries out, good to fight yeast infections.
Cooking time approx. 20 min
Calories p. portion: 96
4 portions
Allergens: M

Quantity of ingredients:
Olive oil 2 table spoons / 35g. (yes)
Cucumber 2 pieces / 400g. (yes)
Water 2 cup / 500g. (yes)
Sage 3 leaves / 3g. (yes)
Mustard 1/2 teaspoon / 0,5g. (yes)
Coriander 1 pinch / 1g. (yes)
Cardamom 1 pinch / 1g. (yes)
Salt 1 pinch / 1g. (little)

Cooking instructions:
Heat oil and roast short the small cucumbers. Add Mustard seeds, coriander, cardamom and salt. Add water. Simmer for 10-15 min. Puree and decorate with fresh chopped sage.

9.21 Fish soup with rosemary

Promotes spleen and liver, reduces blood pressure, strengthens immune system, prevents cancer, reduces radiation damage, has little cholesterol and is protein rich, improves blood circulation, increases appetite. Antioxidant, forcing spleen, dissolves stagnation.
Cooking time approx. 30 min
Calories p. portion: 271
4 portions
Allergens: DLO

Quantity of ingredients:
Basic recipe for a fish soup 2 cup / 500g. (yes)
Rosemary 1/2 bunch / 7g. (yes)
Onion (spring onion) 1 piece / 20g. (yes)
Olive oil 2 table spoons / 35g. (yes)
Fish pieces mixed (fresh water) 5/8 lbs - 8oz / 250g. (yes)
Carrot 1 piece / 120g. (yes)
Parsnip 1 piece / 180g. (yes)
Celery root 1 slice / 20g. (yes)
Salt 1 pinch / 1g. (little)
Peppercorns 2 pieces / 1g. (yes)
Garlic 1 clove / 3g. (yes)

Cooking instructions:
Fry the onion and garlic in oil. Add fish broth. Add diced carrots, parsnips and celery. Season with salt and peppercorns. Simmer the soup on a low heat for 25 minutes.
Wash the fish, drizzle with lemon juice, divide into pieces and add to the soup with the pink rosemary. Cook for 5 min on low heat.
Add the chives and parsley and season the soup with the salt.

9.22 Fish soup with white wine, laurel and marjoram

Strengthens the kidneys, promotes watering, promotes spleen and liver, reduces blood pressure, improves blood circulation, improves medication effect, stimulates appetite, reduces blood pressure.
Cooking time approx. 45 min
Calories p. portion: 200
3 portions
Allergens: DLO

Quantity of ingredients:
Onion (spring onion) 2 pieces / 40g. (yes)
Garlic 1 clove / 2g. (yes)
Basic recipe for a fish soup 2 cup / 500g. (yes)
Carrot 1 piece / 60g. (yes)
Parsnip 1 piece / 100g. (yes)
Celery root 1 slice / 60g. (yes)
Salt 1 pinch / 1g. (little)
Peppercorns 2 pieces / 1g. (yes)
Lemon 1/4 piece / 10g. (yes)
White wine 1/2 cup / 125g. (little)
Bay leaf 2 leaves / 1g. (yes)
Rosemary 1 teaspoon / 2g. (yes)
Chives 1 teaspoon (chopped) / 3g. (yes)
Parsley 1 teaspoon (chopped) / 3g. (yes)

Cooking instructions:
Fry the onion and garlic in oil until translucent. Add fish broth. Add the diced carrot, parsnip and celery. Season with salt and peppercorns. Simmer the soup on a low heat for 25 minutes.
Wash the fish, drizzle with lemon juice, divide into pieces and add to the soup with the wine, the bay leaves and the marjoram. Cook for 5 min on low heat. Add the chives and parsley and season the soup with the salt.

9.23 Fried asparagus with rocket

Diuretic, improves blood circulation, prevents cancer, stimulates digestion, forcing spleen, promotes weight loss. Good to fight immunodeficiency, loss of appetite, arteriosclerosis, flatulence, bladder weakness, anemia, high blood pressure, depressions, diabetes.
Cooking time approx. 15 min
Calories p. portion: 149
3 portions
Allergens: G

Quantity of ingredients:
Butter organic 1 table spoon / 20g. (yes)
Asparagus (green or white) 1,1 lbs / 500g. (yes)
Pepper (ground) 1 pinch / 0,5g. (yes)
Salt 1 pinch / 1g. (little)
Lemon 1/4 piece / 12g. (yes)
Rucola 2 handful / 30g. (yes)
Potato 3/4 lbs / 300g. (yes)

Cooking instructions:
Melt a piece of butter in a hot pan; cut the peeled asparagus into pieces of 3 to 4 cm, fry for about 10 minutes until tender, but crisp. Sprinkle with freshly ground pepper, salt, add a few drops of lemon juice or finely grated lemon zest, finely shredded rucola leaves.
Cook the potatoes in plenty of salted water, then peel.

9.24 Fruit jelly

Promotes spleen and liver, reduces blood pressure, strengthens immune system. Promotes digestion. Warms stomach and spleen, improves blood circulation. For cholesterol diet.
Cooking time approx. 2 hours and more
Calories p. portion: 60
2 portions
Allergens:

Quantity of ingredients:
Carrot (Early Carrot) 3/4 lbs / 300g. (yes)
Water 6 table spoons / 50g. (yes)
Sugar cane sugar 1 teaspoon / 3g. (recommended)
Gelatin white 1 Leaf / 3g. (yes)
Orange 1/2 piece / 50g. (yes)
Cinnamon ground 1 pinch / 0,2g. (yes)
Corn germ oil 1/2 teaspoon / 2g. (yes)

Cooking instructions:
Thoroughly wash, clean, peel and slice the carrots.
Boil about 6 tablespoons of water in a saucepan, add the carrots and cane sugar and cook over medium heat for 10-15 minutes.

Meanwhile, soak the gelatin in cold water for about 10 minutes.

Squeeze the orange half, mix the juice with the cinnamon and the oil. Crush the hot carrots with the blender and dissolve the gelatine (alternative: use agar-agar) in the hot mush.

Stir in the orange juice. Swirl out a pudding mold (1/4 liter content) with cold water, pour in the carrot sauce and refrigerate in the fridge for about 3 hours.
Tip out before eating and allow to warm to room temperature.

9.25 Fruit juice

Stops diarrhea, promotes digestion, appetizing, harmonizes the stomach, relieves pain, detoxifying, reduces blood pressure, strengthens immune system, prevents cancer, reduces radiation damage.
Cooking time approx. 10 min
Calories p. portion: 176
2 portions
Allergens:

Quantity of ingredients:
Orange 2 pieces / 150g. (yes)
Apple (sweet) 4 pieces / 300g. (recommended)
Carrot 2 pieces / 150g. (yes)
Honey 1 table spoon / 10g. (recommended)

Cooking instructions:
Peel oranges and carrots. Cut all ingredients into cubes so that they fit into the juicer and juice. Sweet with honey.

9.26 Japanese algae soup

Reduces blood pressure, strengthens immune system, prevents cancer, reduces radiation damage. Promotes digestion. Detoxifying and stimulates the immune system.
Cooking time approx. 20 min
Calories p. portion: 47
3 portions
Allergens:

Quantity of ingredients:
Wakame 1 oz / 25g. (yes)
Water 2 cup / 450g. (yes)
Onion (shallot) 1-2 pcs. / 30g. (yes)
Radish (white, green, purple-red) 1/8 lbs - 2oz / 50g. (yes)
Carrot 2 pieces / 180g. (yes)
Miso 2 table spoons / 20g. (yes)
Parsley 2 table spoons / 20g. (yes)
Onion (spring onion) 1 table spoon (sliced)

Cooking instructions:
Soak wakame in water for a few minutes, remove and bring the water to the boil. Add finely chopped onions and wakame, radishes and carrots, cut into thin strips, and simmer for another 10 minutes. Dissolve miso in a little cooled cooking water and add it at the end. Sprinkle with parsley and spring onions.

9.27 Mango banana yoghurt drink ice cold

Good to fight loss of appetite, oral mucosa inflammation. Regulates gastrointestinal function, chronic constipation. Prevents cancer.
Diuretic, forcing spleen.
Cooking time approx. 5 min
Calories p. portion: 121
2 portions
Allergens: G

Quantity of ingredients:
Mango juice 1/2 cup / 100g. (recommended)
Yogurt (natural, 1.5% fat) 1/4 lbs - 4oz / 100g. (yes)
Mineral water 1/2 cup / 100g. (yes)
Banana 1/2 piece / 150g. (recommended)
Acerola fruit nectar or powder 1 teaspoon / 2g. (yes)

Cooking instructions:
Mix all the ingredients and 2-3 ice cubes in a blender.

9.28 Minestrone

Diuretic, Supports urination. Promotes digestion, Helps to digest fat, Supports urination, reduces blood pressure. strengthens immune system.
Cooking time approx. 30 min
Calories p. portion: 211
4 portions
Allergens: GL

Quantity of ingredients:
Onion (shallot) 2 pieces / 40g. (yes)
Sunflower oil 1 teaspoon / 10g. (yes)
Water 2 cup / 480g. (yes)
Carrot 2 pieces / 120g. (yes)
Savoy cabbage / kale Handful / 15g. (yes)
Beans (green, fresh) Handful / 20g. (yes)

Celery sticks 3 pieces / 20g. (yes)
Peas, green 4 table spoons / 30g. (yes)
Zucchini 1 piece / 200g. (yes)
Rice variety any 1 cup / 120g. (yes)
Bay leaf 3 leaves / 1g. (yes)
Sunflower oil 1 table spoon / 10g. (yes)
Salt 1 pinch / 1g. (little)
Tomato 3 pieces / 150g. (yes)
Thyme 1 Twig / 3g. (yes)
Parmesan 2 table spoons / 18g. (yes)
Basil 4 leaves / 2g. (yes)

Cooking instructions:
Fry the onion in oil in a glassy saucepan and add water. Add vegetables, rice and salt and simmer gently. If the vegetables are firm, add tomatoes, a small sprig of thyme, basil and bay leaf and leave to simmer. Serve with Parmesan.

9.29 Oyster mushrooms with asparagus

Forces, reduces inflammation, improves digestion, lowers cholesterol, strengthens kidney, stimulates liver function, improves blood circulation, improves medication effect, increases appetite.
Cooking time approx. 30 min
Calories p. portion: 316
4 portions
Allergens: GH

Quantity of ingredients:
Onion white 1 piece / 50g. (yes)
Butter organic 2 table spoons / 40g. (yes)
Oyster mushroom 3/4 lbs / 300g. (yes)
Sake 2 table spoons / 40g. (yes)
Parsley 2 table spoons / 40g. (yes)
Walnuts 2 table spoons / 60g. (recommended)
Asparagus (green or white) 1,1 lbs / 500g. (yes)
Salt 1 pinch / 1g. (little)
Sugar white 1 pinch / 0,1g. (recommended)
Potato 1 lbs / 500g. (yes)
Salt (herbal) 1 pinch / 1g. (little)

Cooking instructions:
Cook organically grown potatoes with the skin, otherwise prepare peeled boiled potatoes. Boil the asparagus in salted water with a pinch of sugar and salt. (You can cook an old roll that absorbs the bittering substances.) Slightly sauté the chopped onions in a pan in the butter before frying the oyster mushrooms cut into the same pan. Stew 15 minutes, stirring several times. Add the sake, walnuts and parsley and simmer on low heat while you drain the potatoes and asparagus. Finally, sprinkle some herbal salt over it.
If no fresh asparagus is available, asparagus can be used in jars.

9.30 Paprika-tomato rice

Good to fight little cholesterol, diabetes. Low in protein, low fat content, little protein. Forcing spleen, dissolves stagnation, promotes weight loss. Good to fight immunodeficiency, loss of appetite, flatulence, high blood pressure, depressions.
Cooking time approx. 25 min
Calories p. portion: 291
3 portions
Allergens: L

Quantity of ingredients:
Onion white 1 piece / 50g. (yes)
Peppers 4 pieces / 120g. (yes)
Bay leaf 2 pieces / 1g. (yes)
Clove 2 pieces / 1g. (yes)
Basic recipe for a vegetable soup (nutritious) 7/8 lbs / 400g. (yes)
Rice (whole grain) 5/8 oz / 200g. (yes)
Champignon 1/8 lbs - 2oz / 60g. (yes)
Parsley 1/2 oz / 20g. (yes)
Pepper (ground) 1 pinch / 0,2g. (yes)
Peppers (rose peppers) 1 pinch / 0,2g. (yes)
Tomato 1/4 lbs - 4oz / 120g. (yes)

Cooking instructions:
Finely chop the onion. Cut the peppers into fine strips.
Heat margarine in a saucepan, sauté onions and peppers, and rice.
Add the vegetable stock, add cloves and bay leaves and leave to simmer in a closed pot for approx. 20 minutes. Cut the tomato meat into 1 cm cubes and add to the rice 5 minutes before the end of cooking.

9.31 Plums with curd cheese

Cancer preventive effect, dehydrates the body, stimulates digestion and binds fats in the intestine. Good ti fight weakness, belching, diabetes, acute or chronic obstruction of the bowel, skin problems.
Cooking time approx. 10 min
Calories p. portion: 141
2 portions
Allergens: G

Quantity of ingredients:
Plums 1 lbs / 500g. (yes)
Butter organic 1/2 teaspoon / 2g. (yes)
Vanilla 1 pinch / 0,2g. (yes)
Cinnamon ground 1 pinch / 0,2g. (yes)
Coriander 1 pinch / 0,2g. (yes)
Cardamom 1 pinch / 0,2g. (yes)
Lemon juice 1 dash / 1g. (yes)
Cocoa 1 pinch / 0,3g. (yes)
Apple juice (natural cloudy) 1 dash / 3g. (recommended)
Sugar cane sugar 1 teaspoon / 3g. (recommended)
Curd cheese 20% 2 table spoons / 30g. (yes)

Cooking instructions:
Cut plums in half. Steam the plums in a pan in a little butter. Add vanilla, cinnamon and a pinch of cilantro and cardamom.
Add water so that the plums ¼ are covered.
Add lemon juice and a pinch of cocoa. Pour with little pear or apple juice, so that the plums are covered about halfway.
Sweet to taste with whole cane sugar.
Approximately Simmer for 7 minutes on the lightest heat so that the plums are tender but not overcooked.
Arrange plums in a circle on the plate.
In the middle a tablespoon of organic quark (who may like to use sheep milk quark).
Pour little juice of cooked plums over the dessert.

9.32 Porridge with raisins and sake

Strengthens immune system, improves blood circulation, improves medication effect, stimulates appetite, detoxifies the skin, stimulates nerves, frees breathing, increases body temperature, promotes perspiration.
Cooking time approx. 10 min
Calories p. portion: 427
1 portions
Allergens: AGO

Quantity of ingredients:
Oat flakes (whole grain) 8 table spoons / 60g. (yes)
Water 1/2 cup / 125g. (yes)
Cow's milk (whole milk 3.5% fat) 1/2 cup / 125g. (recommended)
Salt 1 pinch / 1g. (little)
Cream, sweet 30% 2 table spoons / 20g. (recommended)
Raisins 1 table spoon / 15g. (yes)
Sake 1 table spoon / 10g. (yes)

Cooking instructions:
Heat water and milk and a pinch of salt till it boils. Sprinkle in 4 tablespoons of coarse rolled oats and cook to a pulp, add 4 tablespoons of fine oatmeal, allow to simmer. Arrange in a preheated bowl and top with cream.
Add raisins and sake.

9.33 Potato cream with herbs and fresh cheese

Good to fight loss of appetite, constipation, bloating and nausea. Improves digestion, supports urination, prevents cancer, forcing spleen, dissolves stagnation, relaxing and reassuring.
Cooking time approx. 25 min
Calories p. portion: 217
2 portions
Allergens: G

Quantity of ingredients:
Potato (mealy) 5/8 lbs - 8oz / 250g. (yes)
Fresh cheese 3 oz / 80g. (yes)
Yogurt (natural, 1.5% fat) 2 table spoons / 45g. (yes)
Chives 1/2 bunch / 50g. (yes)
Basil (fresh) 1 teaspoon / 4g. (yes)
Parsley 1 teaspoon / 4g. (yes)

Dill 1/2 teaspoon / 2g. (yes)
Salt 1 pinch / 1g. (little)
Black caraway 1 pinch / 0,5g. (yes)
Pepper (ground) 1 pinch / 0,5g. (yes)

Cooking instructions:
Softly steam the potatoes in the pan, peel them and press through the potato press.
Mix cream cheese, yoghurt and herbs under the potatoes, season with salt, crushed black cumin and pepper.

9.34 Pumpkin slices with spicy rice

Strengthens lungs and spleen, diuretic, reduces blood glucose, protects liver, for the drainage of the body overweight and high blood pressure, harmonizes liver.
Cooking time approx. 45 min
Calories p. portion: 438
4 portions
Allergens: AG

Quantity of ingredients:
Clarified butter 1/2 teaspoon / 5g. (yes)
Saffron 1 Sachet / 0,1g. (yes)
Turmeric (yellow root) 1 teaspoon / 2g. (yes)
Rice Basmati 1 cup / 120g. (yes)
Water 1 cup / 120g. (yes)
Salt 1/2 teaspoon / 2g. (little)
Pumpkin 6-8 slices / 400g. (yes)
Barley flour 1 cup / 10g. (yes)
Breadcrumbs (wheat bread, bread roll) 1 cup / 10g. (yes)
Salt 1/2 teaspoon / 2g. (little)
Pepper (ground) 1 pinch / 1g. (yes)
Butter organic 1 table spoon / 10g. (yes)
Cream, sweet 30% 1 1/2 cup / 300g. (recommended)
Barley flour 2 table spoons / 20g. (yes)
Chives 2 table spoons / 20g. (yes)
Dill 2 table spoons / 20g. (yes)

Cooking instructions:
Melt the fat in a small saucepan, add saffron and turmeric, lightly roast over medium heat for about 1-2 minutes to allow the aromas to develop (note: the spices should never be burnt). Add the rice for about 2 minutes stir fry, add the salt, stir briefly and add the water, stir and close the pot with a lid. Cook at low to medium heat until the water is almost completely absorbed, then remove from the heat and set aside with the lid still closed and let it swell. Do not stir! When the water is completely absorbed, the rice is ready!

Mix flour, bread crumbs, salt and pepper. Moisten the pumpkin slices with water or mashed egg, turn the slices in the flour mixture and fry gently in butter until golden brown and the pumpkin is soft. Melt the butter in a small saucepan, brown the barley flour in it and remove from heat, add the sour cream, season with salt, pepper, add the chopped herbs and pour the sauce over the fried pumpkin slices. Serve with the rice.

9.35 Radish juice with cane sugar

Promotes digestion, detoxifying (for example alcohol poisoning), improves blood circulation, supports urination, reduces thirst, prevents cancer, strengthens body cells.
Cooking time approx. 15 min
Calories p. portion: 89
1 portions
Allergens:

Quantity of ingredients:
Radish (white, green, purple-red) 1/2 piece / 50g. (yes)
Sugar cane sugar 2 table spoons / 20g. (recommended)

Cooking instructions:
Grate the radish, mix with the cane sugar, let it rest and squeeze out the juice. Take the juice spoon wise.

9.36 Radish with horseradish

Stimulates liver function, detoxifying. Promotes digestion, improves blood circulation, supports urination, reduces thirst.
Cooking time approx. 30 min
Calories p. portion: 196
2 portions
Allergens: GNO

Quantity of ingredients:
Butter organic 1 table spoon / 8g. (yes)
Radish (white, green, purple-red) 1/2 piece / 50g. (yes)
Water 2 table spoons / 10g. (yes)
Lemon juice 2 table spoons / 20g. (yes)
White wine 2 table spoons / 20g. (little)
Pepper powder (hot) 1 pinch / 0,2g. (yes)
Sesame oil 1 teaspoon / 3g. (yes)
Radish horseradish 2 table spoons / 20g. (yes)
Salt 1 pinch / 0,5g. (little)
Parsley 1 Bunch (chopped) / 80g. (yes)
Rice long grain rice 1/2 cup / 60g. (yes)
Water 3 cups / 300g. (yes)
Salt 1 pinch / 0,5g. (little)

Cooking instructions:
In a hot pan melt the butter, sautéed into stripes cut radish. Add cold water, lemon juice, white wine, a pinch of rose paprika and stir in the sesame oil; with 2 - 3 tablespoons fresh grated horseradish (alternatively 1 teaspoon from the glass), salt to taste; Sprinkle with chopped parsley.

Place the rice with the water, salt and cook for about 15 minutes.

9.37 Radish, apple and yogurt fresh food

Stops diarrhea, promotes digestion, appetizing, detoxifying, supports urination, reduces thirst, prevents cancer, strengthens body cells, dissolves stagnation.
Cooking time approx. 10 min
Calories p. portion: 77
2 portions
Allergens: G

Quantity of ingredients:
Yogurt (natural, 3.5% fat) 5 table spoons / 50g. (recommended)
Lemon juice 1/2 teaspoon / 2g. (yes)
Salt 1 pinch / 0,5g. (little)
Pepper white (ground) 1 pinch / 0,1g. (yes)
Radish (white, green, purple-red) 1/4 lbs - 4oz / 100g. (yes)
Apple (sweet) 1 piece / 150g. (recommended)
Parsley 2 table spoons / 18g. (yes)

Cooking instructions:
Mix yoghurt with lemon juice, salt and white pepper.

Wash radish and apple, peel and finely grate. Mix with the yoghurt sauce, let it pass briefly. Sprinkle with chopped parsley.

9.38 Red berry with beaters

Calms stomach, strengthens tendons and bones, supports urination, promotes digestion. Strengthens immune system, activates cell metabolism.
Cooking time approx. 15 min
Calories p. portion: 124
2 portions
Allergens: G

Quantity of ingredients:
Berries of the season 1 1/2 cups / 200g. (recommended)
Grape juice red 1 cup / 200g. (recommended)
Sugar molasses 1 table spoon / 10g. (recommended)
Vanilla 1 pinch / 0,2g. (yes)
Cream (30% fat) 2 table spoons / 20g. (recommended)

Cooking instructions:
Put berries and red fruits (redcurrants, raspberries, strawberries, blackberries and blueberries) in a saucepan. Add half a glass of elderberry juice, half a glass of red wine or red grape juice. Add one tablespoon of sugarcane molasses and a pinch of vanilla. Simmer for a few minutes and serve with a bit of whipped cream.

9.39 Red lentils with avocado and radish

Inflammations, promotes digestion, detoxifying, supports urination, reduces thirst. Strengthens heart and kidney, diuretic, calms the stomach, promotes digestion.
Cooking time approx. 20 min
Calories p. portion: 269
3 portions
Allergens: N

Quantity of ingredients:
Ginger fresh 2 slices / 2g. (yes)
Water 1 1/2 cups / 200g. (yes)
Lentils red 1 cup peeled / 100g. (yes)
Wakame 1 inch / 1g. (yes)
Salt 1 pinch / 0,5g. (little)
Lemon juice 1 dach / 1g. (yes)
Curcuma 1 pinch / 0,3g. (yes)
Avocado 1 piece / 300g. (yes)
Pepper (ground) 1 pinch / 0,2g. (yes)
Pepper powder (hot) 1 pinch / 0,2g. (yes)
Sesame oil 1 dash / 1g. (yes)
Radish (white, green, purple-red) 1 cup / 100g. (yes)

Cooking instructions:
Put in a pot with water, some chopped ginger, peeled red lentils, a piece of wakame or a small amount of hijiki and simmer until the lentils are soft. Season with salt, lemon juice and turmeric.

Meanwhile: place half an avocado per serving on one-third of the plate: add ground pepper, a pinch of salt, a little lemon juice, a pinch of sweet pepper and a little sesame oil.

Put the grated radish on the second plate third.

Fill the lentil dish into the last third of the plate.
Variant: Use radish slices instead of radishes.

9.40 Refreshing cucumber soup with potatoes

Diuretic, detoxifying, suppresses conversion of sugar into fat, lowers cholesterol, prevents cancer, reduces inflammation, improves digestion, lowers cholesterol, dissolves stagnation, improves blood circulation, stimulates appetite.
Cooking time approx. 15 min
Calories p. portion: 148
3 portions
Allergens: GN

Quantity of ingredients:
Sesame oil 1 table spoon / 10g. (yes)
Potato 4 pieces / 300g. (yes)
Onion (spring onion) 3 pieces / 60g. (yes)
Pepper (ground) 1 pinch / 0,5g. (yes)
Nutmeg 1 pinch / 1g. (yes)
Salt 1 pinch / 1g. (little)
Lemon 1/2 piece / 25g. (yes)
Cucumber 2 pieces / 500g. (yes)
Cream, sweet 30% 1 table spoon / 10g. (recommended)
Dill 1 table spoon / 15g. (yes)

Cooking instructions:
Sauté sesame oil, chopped potatoes, plenty of spring onions in a hot pot; add pepper, a little nutmeg, salt, lemon juice, hot water, diced cucumber; simmer for about 10 minutes and then puree; add some sweet cream as you like, fresh dill.
Variation: Add a little chili, oregano, thyme or rosemary to soften the cooling effect.

9.41 Rhubarb cake with sprinkles

Laxative, antipyretic, good to fight flatulence, brittle nails and hair. Relieves pain, detoxifying, against dry skin, acne, eczema.
Cooking time approx. 1 1/2 hours
Calories p. portion: 476
8 portions
Allergens: AG

Quantity of ingredients:
Wheat flour 7/8 lbs / 400g. (yes)
Cow's milk (whole milk 3.5% fat) 1 cup / 200g. (recommended)
Yeast 1 oz / 30g. (yes)
Honey 2 teaspoons / 5g. (recommended)
Sunflower oil 2 teaspoons / 5g. (yes)
Lemon peel 1 piece / 3g. (yes)
Salt 1 pinch / 1g. (little)
Rhubarb 2,2 lbs / 800g. (yes)
Margarine 1/4 lbs - 4oz / 120g. (yes)
Wheat flour 3/4 lbs / 300g. (yes)
Vanilla sugar natural 2 pinches / 1g. (yes)
Cinnamon ground 2 pinches / 1g. (yes)
Honey 5 table spoons / 50g. (recommended)

Cooking instructions:
Mix flour, grated lemon peel and salt.
Heat milk gently and mix with yeast and honey.
Then add the flour mixture and the oil and knead vigorously. Cover the dough and let it rise in a warm place until it reaches twice the amount. (about 30 minutes)
For the sprinkles, mix flour with vanilla and cinnamon, then add honey and margarine and crumble to a crumbly mass. Keep the sprinkles dough cool.
Lay out a baking sheet with parchment paper.
Knead the dough for the bottom again, roll it out, place it on the baking sheet and let it rise for another 10 minutes.
Clean the rhubarb, wash it, halve lengthwise and cut into pieces of approx. 3 cm. Spread the pieces on the rolled out dough and crumble the sprinkles over the cake.
Place the cake in the preheated oven at 175 ° C and bake for about 40 minutes.

9.42 Ribbon noodles with leaf spinach

Promotes digestion, improves blood circulation, forcing spleen and intestine, improves pancreatic function, Good to fight loss of appetite, flatulence, inflammatory bowel disease, obesity, stomach ulcers, stomach cramps, rheumatism, heartburn, twelffinger intestinal ulcers.
Cooking time approx. 45 min
Calories p. portion: 722
2 portions
Allergens: ACG

Quantity of ingredients:
Spinach 5/8 lbs - 8oz / 250g. (yes)
Salt 1 pinch / 1g. (little)
Noodles (wheat, ribbon noodles) with egg 5/8 oz / 200g. (yes)
Olive oil 1 table spoon / 15g. (yes)
Onion (spring onion) 1 piece / 20g. (yes)
Cream, sweet 30% 1/2 cup / 100g. (recommended)
Créme fraiche cheese 1/2 teaspoon / 6g. (yes)
Thyme dried 1/2 teaspoon / 2g. (yes)
Basil (fresh) 1/2 teaspoon / 2g. (yes)
Oregano dried 1/2 teaspoon / 2g. (yes)
Nutmeg 1 pinch / 0,5g. (yes)
Pepper (ground) 1 pinch / 0,5g. (yes)

Parmesan 1/2 oz / 20g. (yes)
Pine nuts 1 table spoon / 15g. (yes)
Black caraway 1 pinch / 1g. (yes)

Cooking instructions:
Put the dripping wet spinach together with a little salt for 3 minutes in a pot, then drain in a sieve. Then finely cut.
Boil tagliatelle in plenty of salted water.
Heat the oil in a skillet and fry the spring onions rings. Add cream, crème fraiche, thyme, basil, oregano and nutmeg. Stir in the sauce while stirring. Add the spinach, heat briefly, season with nutmeg, salt and pepper.
Drain pasta and mix with the spinach. Season with salt and pepper.
Portion noodles and serve with parmesan and pine nuts. Sprinkle the black cumin over it.

9.43 Rice congee with carrots and fennel

Worms, forcing spleen, relieves constipation, stimulates nerves, detoxifying, reduces inflammation, improves blood circulation, reduces blood pressure, strengthens immune system, prevents cancer, reduces radiation damage.
Cooking time approx. 2 hours and more
Calories p. portion: 131
3 portions
Allergens: G

Quantity of ingredients:
Basic recipe for a rice soup (Congee) 2 cup / 500g. (yes)
Carrot 2 pieces / 100g. (yes)
Fennel 1 piece / 250g. (yes)
Butter organic 1 teaspoon / 3g. (yes)
Cardamom 1/2 teaspoon / 1g. (yes)

Cooking instructions:
Cook rice congee according to basic recipe.
Clean and cut carrots and fennel.
When carrots and fennel are cooked from the beginning, they serve wholesomeness. If added shortly before the end of the cooking time, taste and vitamins are retained.
Refine with butter and cardamom before serving.

9.44 Rice congee with crushed walnuts

Good to fight blood circulation disorders, high blood pressure, a headache, for the drainage of the body overweight and high blood pressure. Dissolves stones. Warms stomach and spleen, improves blood circulation. Antipyretic.
Cooking time approx. 2 hours and more
Calories p. portion: 406
2 portions
Allergens: H

Quantity of ingredients:
Basic recipe for a rice soup (Congee) 4 cups / 500g. (yes)
Sugar cane sugar 2 table spoons / 20g. (recommended)
Walnuts 1 cup / 70g. (recommended)
Cinnamon ground 1 pinch / 0,2g. (yes)

Cooking instructions:
Cook the basic recipe for rice soup (congee)
Note: The crushed walnuts can be cooked from the beginning.
Variation: Refine with sweet or spicy ingredients as you like. In particular, cinnamon, cloves, and ginger increase the warming effect and wholesomeness.

9.45 Rice congee with honey pear and black sesame

Promotes digestion, supports urination, good to fight blood circulation disorders, thromboses, risk of embolism, high blood pressure, a headache, heart attack and stroke.
Cooking time approx. 10 min - 3 hours
Calories p. portion: 158
2 portions
Allergens: N

Quantity of ingredients:
Basic recipe for a rice soup (Congee) 1 1/2 cups / 240g. (yes)
Pear 2 pieces / 300g. (recommended)
Sesame, black 1 teaspoon / 3g. (yes)

Cooking instructions:
Cook rice congee according to basic recipe.
Fill pot with 3 cm of water and heat till it boils. Quarter the pears (with the skin and seeds) and simmer them covered with black sesame for 10 minutes. Mix with the rice.

9.46 Rice noodle soup with shiitake mushrooms

Very light and powerful. Strengthens the immune system.
Cooking time approx. 20 min
Calories p. portion: 66
2 portions
Allergens: L

Quantity of ingredients:
Rice noodles 2 handful / 20g. (yes)
Shiitake, dried 4-6 pieces / 5g. (yes)
Basic recipe for a vegetable soup (nutritious) 1 1/2 cups / 240g. (yes)
Chinese cabbage 1 cup / 60g. (yes)
Lovage 1 teaspoon / 3g. (yes)
Miso 2 table spoons / 18g. (yes)

Cooking instructions:
Soak rice noodles and shiitake mushrooms separately in cold water.
Heat the vegetable broth and add the soaked shiitake mushrooms cut
into strips and simmer gently. Cut Chinese cabbage into noodles, add
lovage green and rice noodles and let it steep for a while. Before
serving, stir in Miso dissolved in a little cooled water. Recommendation:
Suitable at the beginning of each meal, also for breakfast

9.47 Rice soup with grated carrots and fresh herbs

Diuretic, warming the body from the inside, expands blood vessels,
strengthens the muscles, regulates internal organs functions, reduces
blood pressure, strengthens immune system, prevents cancer, reduces
radiation damage. Promotes digestion.
Cooking time approx. 5 min
Calories p. portion: 131
4 portions
Allergens: EG

Quantity of ingredients:
Rice wild (nature rice) 1 cup / 100g. (yes)
Water 6 cups / 700g. (yes)
Carrot 1 piece / 100g. (yes)
Soy sauce 1 dash / 2g. (yes)
Butter organic 1 teaspoon / 3g. (yes)
Ground 1 pinch / 0,3g. (yes)
Curcuma 1 pinch / 0,2g. (yes)
Herbs various 1 teaspoon (chopped) / 3g. (yes)

Cooking instructions:
In a portion of rice congee according to basic recipe, softly cook a grated carrot, add butter and soy sauce.
Sprinkle with fresh herbs.

Spices and herbs: black cumin, turmeric, cardamom, parsley, sage, thyme, basil, rosemary.

Winter: parsnip, celery, onion, leek, pumpkin
Summer: tomatoes, zucchini, spring onion, radishes, arugula.

9.48 Rice with stewed vegetables

Reduces blood pressure, strengthens immune system, prevents cancer, reduces radiation damage, extremely low fat content, good to fight blood circulation disorders, thrombose, risk of embolism, a headache, heart attack and stroke. Is diuretic.
Cooking time approx. 20 min
Calories p. portion: 166
2 portions
Allergens: L

Quantity of ingredients:
Rice variety any 1/2 cup / 60g. (yes)
Water 3 cups / 300g. (yes)
Lemon peel 1 piece / 3g. (yes)
Water 1/2 cup / 0g. (yes)
Carrot 2 pieces / 180g. (yes)
Celery sticks 1/2 piece / 5g. (yes)
Champignon 1/2 cup / 50g. (yes)
Cress 2 table spoons / 20g. (yes)
Linseed oil 1 dash / 3g. (yes)

Cooking instructions:
Cook rice according to basic recipe with a piece of lemon peel.
Steam chopped carrots, celery and mushrooms until soft.
Then sprinkle with cress. Then add a dash of high quality cold oil.

9.49 Ricepudding

Regulates gastrointestinal function. Strengthens spleen and stomach, strengthens the muscles. Vitamin C rich.
Cooking time approx. 2 hours and more
Calories p. portion: 316
1 portions
Allergens: G

Quantity of ingredients:
Cow's milk (whole milk 3.5% fat) 3/4 cup - 6 oz / 200g. (recommended)
Rice round grain 1 oz / 25g. (yes)
Banana 1/4 lbs - 4oz / 100g. (recommended)
Red berry (without sugar) 2 teaspoons / 4g. (yes)

Cooking instructions:
Heat half of the milk till it boils in a small saucepan.
Sprinkle the rice and cook on low heat for about 15 minutes.
Peel the banana, finely grate with the blender and add the beetroot juice.
Mix the banana bran under the hot rice.
Pour a pudding mold (about 1/4 liter of contents) in cold water.
Fill the banana rice in the mold and let the pudding swell at room temperature.
After about 3 hours it is solid and can be toppled.
Take the remaining milk as a drink.

9.50 Soup with cucumbers and tomatoes

Diuretic, detoxifying, suppresses conversion of sugar into fat, lowers cholesterol. Promotes digestion, helps to digest fat, supports urination, reduces blood pressure, calms nerves and stomach.
Cooking time approx. 10 min
Calories p. portion: 137
2 portions
Allergens: CO

Quantity of ingredients:
Cucumber 1 piece / 300g. (yes)
Tomato 4 pieces (very ripe) / 200g. (yes)
Onion white 1 piece / 50g. (yes)
Peppers 1/2 piece (green) / 10g. (yes)
Salt 1 pinch / 0,5g. (little)
Vinegar (Apple vinegar) 1 dash / 2g. (yes)

Water 1 cup / 120g. (yes)
Chicken egg 2 pieces / 120g. (yes)

Cooking instructions:
Puree all ingredients in the blender. Cool in the fridge. When serving, sprinkle with chopped breadcrumbs and finely chopped boiled egg.

9.51 Spring salad

Blood-forming, blood detoxifying, diuretic, good to fight stomach discomfort, improves digestion, diarrhea, helps to digest fat, supports urination, reduces blood pressure, detoxifying, reduces inflammation, diuretic.
Cooking time approx. 10 min
Calories p. portion: 162
4 portions
Allergens: AEMN

Quantity of ingredients:
Sorrel 3/8 lbs - 6oz / 150g. (yes)
Dandelion (young plants) 1/4 lbs - 4oz / 100g. (yes)
Mung bean sprouting 0,2 lbs / 75g. (yes)
Cress 1/4 lbs - 4oz / 100g. (yes)
Chives 1 Bunch / 50g. (yes)
Tomato 2 pieces / 100g. (yes)
Parsley 1 Bunch / 50g. (yes)
Sesame paste (Tahini) 2 table spoons / 16g. (yes)
Soy sauce 1 dash / 3g. (yes)
Mustard 1/2 teaspoon / 2g. (yes)
White bread (wheat bread) 6 slices / 120g. (yes)

Cooking instructions:
Wash all salad´s, mix and prepare the sauce as follows:
Mix tahini with mustard and balsamic vinegar, tamari, olive oil, chives and half of parsley. Pour the sauce over the salad and sprinkle the remaining parsley just before serving.
Serve with the white bread.

9.52 Summer Salad

Promotes digestion, helps to digest fat, forcing spleen, supports urination, reduces blood pressure. Detoxifying, prevents cancer.
Cooking time approx. 10 min
Calories p. portion: 281
1 portions
Allergens: GMNO

Quantity of ingredients:
Rucola Handful / 15g. (yes)
Radicchio 1 head / 30g. (yes)
Tomato 15 pieces (diced) / 100g. (yes)
Olive oil 1 table spoon / 10g. (yes)
Olives 2 table spoons / 16g. (yes)
Vinegar Aceto Balsamico 1 table spoon / 10g. (yes)
Mustard medium hot 2 teaspoons / 5g. (yes)
Sesame paste (Tahini) 1 teaspoon / 2g. (yes)
Parmesan 2 table spoons / 20g. (yes)
Salt 1 pinch / 0,5g. (little)
Pepper (ground) 1 pinch / 0,2g. (yes)
Rosemary 2 teaspoons / 3g. (yes)

Cooking instructions:
Wash the salad, pluck it small and arrange it in a bowl.
Sauce: Put the oil, the balsamic vinegar, the mustard and the tahini in a glass with a lid and shake well. Season the dressing with salt and pepper. Mix the salad with the salad dressing and the olives, sprinkle with parmesan and finally with rosemary.

9.53 Sweet-savory barley salad

Diuretic, forcing spleen, supports urination, relaxes. Astringent, antibacterial, invigorating, calming.
Cooking time approx. 25 min
Calories p. portion: 511
2 portions
Allergens: AGHO

Quantity of ingredients:
Water 5/8 oz / 50g. (yes)
Barley 1/4 lbs - 4oz / 100g. (yes)
Apple (sour) 2 pieces / 300g. (recommended)
Grapes red Handful / 20g. (yes)

Dates dried 2 table spoons (gutted) / 20g. (yes)
Almond 1 table spoon / 10g. (yes)
Curry 1 pinch / 0,2g. (yes)
Salt 1 pinch / 0,5g. (little)
Lemon juice 1 piece / 20g. (yes)
Lemon peel 1/4 piece / 2g. (yes)
Cocoa 1 pinch / 0,5g. (yes)
Cream, sweet 30% 1/2 cup / 100g. (recommended)

Cooking instructions:
Boil the barley in water. Mix cooked barley, 2 sweet chopped apples, a handful of red grapes, about 80 g of pitted dates, about 50 g of chopped almonds, some curry, a pinch of salt, juice of 1 lemon, grated lemon zest, some cocoa.
Leave for 1 hour; Lift 100 ml of whipped cream underneath.
Recommendation: in the summer as a refreshing evening meal.

9.54 Tofu-Black Bean Chili with Rice

Supports urination, lowers cholesterol, prevents arteriosclerosis, for the drainage of the body overweight and high blood pressure.
Cooking time approx. 45 min
Calories p. portion: 344
4 portions
Allergens: AEL

Quantity of ingredients:
Rapeseed oil 1/4 cup / 60g. (yes)
Onion white 2 pieces / 120g. (yes)
Peppers 1 piece / 20g. (yes)
Pepper Cayenne 1 pinch / 0,5g. (yes)
Coriander 1 teaspoon / 2g. (yes)
Thyme 1 teaspoon / 2g. (yes)
Clove 1 teaspoon / 2g. (yes)
Spelled wholemeal flour 2 table spoons / 16g. (yes)
Sherry (whine) 1 table spoon / 8g. (little)
Soy Tofu 5/8 lbs - 8oz / 250g. (yes)
Black beans 2 cans (400g) / 400g. (yes)
Basic recipe for a chicken soup (warming) 1 1/2 cups / 300g. (yes)
Bay leaf 1 piece / 0,2g. (yes)
Garlic 6 pieces / 8g. (yes)
Water 6 cups / 400g. (yes)
Rice Basmati 1 cup / 120g. (yes)

Cooking instructions:
Heat the oil at medium temperature in a large saucepan, add onions, paprika and chili powder and fry for 2 minutes until the onions are glassy. Add the remaining spices, stirring constantly, stirring until the aroma rises.
Dust the flour, fry for 2 minutes and make sure that the paste-like spice mixture does not burn.
Deglaze with sherry, add the black beans (tin) and mix with the spices. Add the chicken broth, add the bay leaf and stir in the chopped garlic. Simmer the beans for 30 minutes and add some chicken stock if needed.
Cook the tofu cubes during the last 10 minutes. The tofu can easily disintegrate and should therefore be lifted very gently with a wooden spoon. Finally, pick out the bay leaf and serve the tofu black bean chili with rice.

9.55 Tsampa with jam or fruit compote

Promotes spleen, diuretic, supports urination, relaxes, stops diarrhea, promotes digestion, appetizing.
Cooking time approx. 5 min
Calories p. portion: 280
1 portions
Allergens: AGO

Quantity of ingredients:
Tsampa (roasted barley flour) 2 table spoons / 30g. (yes)
Water 6-8 table spoons / 70g. (yes)
Butter organic 1/2 teaspoon / 2g. (yes)
Strawberry jam 1 table spoon / 7g. (yes)
Sunflower seeds 2 teaspoons / 14g. (yes)
Apple (sweet) 1 piece grated / 120g. (recommended)

Cooking instructions:
Pour tsampa with boiling water and stir with a spoon until a porridge is formed.
Add butter, jam, sunflower seeds and grated apple.
Sweet to taste with honey, whole cane sugar, or barley malt.
Spices and herbs: fresh mint, vanilla or cocoa, anise, cinnamon

Summer: jam or compote of your choice
Winter: nuts and apple or pear

9.56 Vanilla pudding

Helps to fight constipation.
Cooking time approx. 10 min
Calories p. portion: 254
2 portions
Allergens: G

Quantity of ingredients:
Cow's milk (whole milk 3.5% fat) 2 cups / 500g. (recommended)
Pudding powder vanilla 1 package / 37g. (yes)
Sugar white 1 table spoon / 12g. (recommended)

Cooking instructions:
Give 3-5 tablespoons of milk into a cup, bring the rest in a pot to boil.
Pour the powdered pudding into the cup and stir until free of lumpy. As
soon as the milk boils, add the mixture and simmer under low heat for
about 3 minutes. Divide into prepared bowls.

9.57 Vitamin drink

Regulates gastrointestinal function, promotes spleen and liver, reduces
blood pressure, strengthens immune system, prevents cancer, reduces
radiation damage, supports urination, quenches thirst, calms the
stomach, prevents cancer.
Cooking time approx. 5 min
Calories p. portion: 172
3 portions
Allergens:

Quantity of ingredients:
Orange juice 1 cup / 300g. (recommended)
Carrot 5/8 oz / 200g. (yes)
Banana 2 pieces / 300g. (recommended)
Kiwi 1 piece / 20g. (yes)

Cooking instructions:
Chop oranges, carrots, bananas and kiwi and finely puree with the
blender.

9.58 Warming carrot soup

Strengthens and warms, reduces blood pressure, strengthens immune system, prevents cancer, reduces radiation damage, strengthens gastrointestinal function.
Cooking time approx. 30 min
Calories p. portion: 133
3 portions
Allergens: HL

Quantity of ingredients:
Carrot 4 pieces / 250g. (yes)
Walnut oil 2 table spoons / 20g. (yes)
Onion (shallot) 2 pieces / 40g. (yes)
Anise (Common Fennel) 1/2 teaspoon / 1g. (yes)
Nutmeg 1 pinch / 1g. (yes)
Ginger fresh 1/2 teaspoon / 1g. (yes)
Salt 1 pinch / 1g. (little)
Basic recipe for a vegetable soup (nutritious) 2 cup / 500g. (yes)
Parsley 1 table spoon / 10g. (yes)

Cooking instructions:
Heat walnut oil in a hot pot and fry onions; steam the carrots in it; add anise, nutmeg, a little ginger, salt and sauté everything; add water or vegetable- or meat stock; cook everything soft and then puree; fold in parsley at the end.

Recommendation: Suitable for the cold season, especially if you use meat broth as a liquid for infusion.

9.59 Wheat semolina with olives-herb-sauce and salad

Protects the digestive system. Detoxifying, affects anorexia, good to fight flatulence, inflammatory bowel disease, obesity, gout, stomach ulcers, stomach cramps, rheumatism, heartburn. Dissolves stagnation, relieves fatigue.
Cooking time approx. 15 min
Calories p. portion: 245
3 portions
Allergens: ACGL

Quantity of ingredients:
Cream, sweet 30% 1/8 lbs - 2oz / 40g. (recommended)
Water 1/3 cup / 65g. (yes)
Wheat semolina 1/4 lbs - 4oz / 100g. (yes)
Chicken egg 1 piece / 60g. (yes)
Pepper (ground) 1 pinch / 0,5g. (yes)
Lemon peel 1 pinch / 1g. (yes)
Onion white 1 piece / 60g. (yes)
Olive oil 1 teaspoon / 2g. (yes)
Chives 1 table spoon / 7g. (yes)
Basic recipe for a vegetable soup (nutritious) 2 cups / 500g. (yes)
Lettuce 2 handful / 30g. (yes)
Olive oil 1 teaspoon / 3g. (yes)
Lemon juice 1 teaspoon / 3g. (yes)
Oregano fresh 1 teaspoon / 2g. (yes)

Cooking instructions:
Mix cream and water and heat till it boils. Stir in the wheat semolina and
cook to a thick porridge and remove from heat. Whisk the egg and stir
in, season with pepper and grated lemon zest. Form with 2 coffee
spoons, dumplings and leave to stir in the slightly boiling vegetable
stock until the dumplings float up.
Chop the onion and roast it in olive oil in a pan. Pour the semolina
dumplings into the pan and sprinkle with finely chopped chives.

Wash salad and cut into thin strips. Season with olive oil, lemon juice
and oregano.

9.60 Whole milk cereal mash

Reduces Inflammation, antiallergic, has a stabilizing effect on the blood
circulation, lowers blood glucose and cholesterol.
Cooking time approx. 20 min
Calories p. portion: 205
1 portions
Allergens: AG

Quantity of ingredients:
Cow's milk (whole milk 3.5% fat) 3/4 cup - 6 oz / 200g. (recommended)
Water 1/4 cup / 50g. (yes)
Spelled flakes 1/2 oz / 20g. (yes)
Fruit mix juice 1/2 oz / 20g. (recommended)

Cooking instructions:
Boil the milk with the wholegrain flakes and let it swell. Add the pureed fruit.

Switch between wheat, oats and wholemeal spelled flakes, as well as the fruits. So you get a variety of flavors.

10 Effects of food

10.1 Use ingredients: recommendable

Acai powder
Apple (sour)
Apple (sweet)
Apple juice (natural cloudy)
Apple puree
Apricot
Apricot nectar
Apricots juice
Banana
Banana (cooking banana)
Berries of the season
Berry juice
Bitter Herb liqueur
Bitter Lemon
Cherry compote
Cherry juice
Clementines
Compote (fruits of the season)
Cow's milk (whole milk 3.5% fat)
Cream (30% fat)
Cream 10% coffee cream
Cream sour 30%
Cream, sweet 30%
Currant juice (black)
Fox nut, gorgon nut, makhana
Fructose (glucose)

Fruit mix juice
Grape juice red
Grape juice white
Hibiscus
Honey
Kudzu
Lily bulbs
Mango juice
Maple syrup
Mascarpone cheese
Orange juice
Pear
Pear juice
Sour cream 15% fat
Sour milk
Sugar - icing sugar
Sugar brown
Sugar candy white
Sugar cane sugar
Sugar molasses
Sugar palm sugar
Sugar white
Supplementary nutrition
Walnuts
Walnuts roasted
Yogurt (natural, 3.5% fat)

10.2 Use ingredients: yes

Acerola fruit nectar or powder
Adzuki beans
Agar agar (kelp)
Agave nectar
Agrimony
Almond
Almond marzipan
Almond milk
Almond puree
Aloe juice
Amaranth
Amaranth Pops
Anchovy / Sardine
Angelica root
Anise (Common Fennel)
Apricot dried
Apricot jam
Apricots
Arrowroot
Artichoke

Asparagus (green or white)
Aubergine
Avocado
Baking powder
Balm
Bamboo shoots
Banchatee (green tea)
barberry
Barley
Barley flour
Barley grass powder
Barley grouts
Barley malt
Barley not peeled
Basic recipe for a beef soup
Basic recipe for a beef soup (warming)
Basic recipe for a chicken soup (warming)
Basic recipe for a duck soup
Basic recipe for a fish soup

Basic recipe for a rice soup (Congee)
Basic recipe for a vegetable soup (nutritious)
Basil
Basil (fresh)
Batavia
Bay leaf
Bean oil
Beans (green, fresh)
Bearberry leaf
Beef bone marrow
Beef fillet
Beef heart
Beef heart (calf)
Beef kidney
Beef liver
Beef lungs (calf)
Beef meat
Beef meat (calf)
Beef meatbones
Beef Oxtail pieces
Beef soup meat
Beef stomach
Beer (alcohol-free)
Beer (alcohol-reduced)
Bitter orange peel
Black beans
Black caraway
Black fungus mushroom
Black tea
Blackberry dried (unripe fruit)
Blackberry jam
Blackberry leaves
Blackberry´s
Black-eyed peas
Blackthorn (Sloe)
Blue mallow tee
Blueberry
Blueberry dried
Blueberry jam
Blueberry juice
Bocksdorn fruits (Fructus Lycii, Goji, goji berry dried
Boletus mushroom
Borage
Borage oil
Boxhorn clover seeds
Brazil nuts
Bread roll
Bread with carob kernel flour
Breadcrumbs (wheat bread, bread roll)
Brie cheese
Broad beans (thick beans)
Broccoli

Brussels sprouts
Buckbean
Buckwheat
Buckwheat (roasted) Kasha
Buckwheat whole grain
Bulgur (cereals)
Burdock root tea
Bush beans
Butter (half fat)
Butter beans white
Butter organic
Buttermilk
Calamari
Camembert
Cantaloupe
Capers in olive oil
Carambola (Star fruit)
Cardamom
Carob flour, St. john's bread
Carp
Carrot
Carrot (Early Carrot)
Carrot juice without sugar
Cashews
Cauliflower
Caviar
Celery root
Celery sticks
Cereal coffee
Chamomile
Chamomile tea
Champignon
Channa-Dal
Chanterelle
Chard
Chenpi (chinese tangerine bowl)
Cherry
Cherry (sour)
Chervil
Chervil dried
Chestnut puree
Chestnuts
Chicken Blood
Chicken egg
Chicken egg white
Chicken heart
Chicken liver
Chicken meat
Chicken stomach
Chicken yolk
Chickpeas
Chickweed
Chicory
Chili (pod or ground)

Chinese cabbage
Chinese pearl barley
Chives
Chlorella (fresh water)
Chocolate
Chocolate (Diabetic)
Chrysanthemum blossom tea
Cinnamon ground
Cinnamon sticks
Clarified butter
Clementine
Clove
Cocoa
Coconut fat
Coconut flakes
Coconut grated
Coconut meat
Coconut milk
Cod
Codfish
Coffee
Coix (seeds) YiYi Ren
Cola drink
Cooking oil
Coriander
Coriander (fresh)
Corn
Corn (fast polenta)
Corn (roasted)
Corn flour
Corn germ oil
Corn Grease (Polenta)
Corn silk tea
Corn starch
Cottage cheese
Couscous
Cow's milk (1.5% fat)
Crab
Cranberries
Cranberry
Cranberry
Cranberry jam
Cranberry juice
Cream sour 10%
Cream sour 20%
Creamer
Créme fraiche cheese
Cress
Crispbread
Crucian
Cucumber
Cucumber (bitter)
Cucumber (spicy cucumber)
Cumin (Caraway seed)

Curcuma
Curd cheese 20%
Curd cheese 40%
Currant (black)
Currant (red)
Currant (white)
Currant jam (black)
Currant jam (red)
Currants (black)
Currants (red)
Curry
Curry paste red
Daisy
Dandelion (young plants)
Dandelion juice
Dandelionroots tea
Dashi
Dates dried
Dates red
Deer meat
Deer meat
Deer's Bones
Deer's kidneys
Dill
Duck (heart)
Duck (slaughtered)
Ducks egg
Dulse (seaweed)
Dyer's broom herb
Edam cheese
Eel
Elderberries
Elderberry blossom tee
Emmental cheese
Endive salad
Evening primrose oil
Fennel
Fennel seeds ground
Fennel tea
Fenugreek (Trigonella foenum-
graecum)
Feta cheese
Feta cheese
Fig
Fig dried
Fish innards
Fish pieces mixed (fresh water)
Fish remains
Fish sauce
Flounder
Flower pollen
French beans
Fresh cheese
Fresh cheese from soya

Fresh cheese with herbs
Freshwater crab
Freshwater fish
Fruit tea
Gail plum
Galangal
Garam Masala powder
Garlic
Gelatin white
Gelee Royal
Gentian root
Gentian root tea
Ginger fresh
Ginger oil
Ginger powder
Ginkgo fruit
Ginseng
Ginseng root
Goat
Goat and sheep's blood
Goat and sheep's brain
Goat and sheep's liver
Goat and sheep's milk
Goat and sheep's stomach
Goat cheese
Goose
Goose blood
Goose egg
Goose fat
Goose parts
Gooseberry
Gorgonzola
Gouda cheese
Gourd
Grapefruit (Pomelo)
Grapefruit dried peel
Grapefruit juice
Grapes red
Grapes white
Grapeseed oil
Grass carp
Green spelt
Green tea
Greengage
Ground
Ground caraway
Guava
Halibut (Flatfish)
Hawthorn
Hazelnuts
Herbal tea mix
Herbs bitter
Herbs of Provence
Herbs various

Herbs wild
Herring
Hibiscus tea
Hijiki
Hokkaido pumpkin
Hop
Horehound leaves
Horse meat
Hyssop
Iceberg lettuce
Jasmine blossoms tee
Jellyfish
Juniper berry
Kaki plum
Kalmus
Kefir
Kidney beans (red)
King Solomon's-seal
Kiwi
Kohlrabi
Kombu seaweed (Saccharina japonica)
Kukicha tea
Kumquats
Ladyfingers
Lamb bones
Lamb kidneys
Lamb liver
Lamb meat
Lamb shoulder
Lamb's lettuce
Lamb's lettuce
Lavender blossoms
Leaf salads (bitter)
Leek
Lemon
Lemon Balm (dried)
Lemon Balm (fresh)
Lemon juice
Lemon peel
Lemongrass
Lentils
Lentils black
Lentils red
Lentils yellow
Lettuce
Licorice root tea
Lima beans
Lime
Lime blossom tea
Linseed
Linseed (crushed)
Linseed oil
Liver smoothing tea
Lobster

Longane
Loquate / Japanese medlar
Lotus roots
Lotus seeds
Lovage
Lovage seeds
Luo Han Guo fruit
Lychee
Lychee in Preserved
Lye roll
Mackerel
Mallow (Malva sylvestris) blossom tea
Malt
Mango
Manioc flour
Mare's milk
Margarine
Margarine (diet)
Marjoram
Mayonnaise 50%
Mayonnaise 80%
Mediterranean fish (cod, plaice, haddock, sea eel, mackerel)
Medlar
Millet
Millet flakes
Mineral water
Mirabelle plum
Miso
Miso black (fermented)
Miso paste (soy bean paste)
Mixed Pickles
Mold cheese
Morel (black, dried)
Morel, dried
Mozzarella
Mu Erh Mushroom
Muesli
Mulberry fruit
Mulled Wine Spice
Mullet
Multi-grain bread (gray bread)
Mung bean
Mung bean sprouting
Mussels
Mustard
Mustard Dijon
Mustard medium hot
Mustard seeds
Mustard sweet
Mutton
Mutton
Nasturtium (nose-twister or nose-tweaker)

Nectarine
Nettles
Noodles (wheat) with egg
Noodles (wheat, lasagne) with egg
Noodles (wheat, ribbon noodles) with egg
Noodles (wheat, spaghetti) with egg
Noodles (whole grain) with egg
Nori, purple seaweed, red algae
Nutmeg
Oat
Oat flakes (whole grain)
Oat flakes roasted
Oat flour
Oat fusion (baby food)
Oat meal
Oat milk
Octopus
Octopus
Okra
Olive oil
Olives
Olives green
Onion (shallot)
Onion (spring onion)
Onion read
Onion white
Orange
Orange blossom
Orange dried peel
Orange grated peel
Orange jam
Orange peel
Oregano dried
Oregano fresh
Oyster mushroom
Oyster shell powder
Oysters
Palm oil
Papaya
Parmesan
Parsley
Parsley root
Parsnip
Passion blossoms tea
Passion fruit
Peaches
Peaches (canned)
Peanut (roasted)
Peanut butter
Peanut oil
Peanuts
Pearl barley
Pearl barley

Peas
Peas, green
Pepper (ground)
Pepper Cayenne
Pepper powder (hot)
Pepper white (ground)
Peppercorns
Peppermint
Peppermint tea
Pepperoni
Pepperoni, red, pitted, halved
Pepperoni, yellow, pitted, halved
Peppers
Peppers (rose peppers)
Peppers (sweet)
Peppers powder
Perch
Pheasant
Pickle
Pig blood
Pigeon
Pigeon egg
Pimento
Pine nuts
Pineapple
Pineapple juice without sugar
Pinto beans speckled
Pistachios
Plaice
Plum
Plum dried
Plums
Pomegranate
Poppy
Pork Bacon
Pork brain
Pork fat (lard)
Pork ham
Pork ham cooked
Pork ham smoked
Pork heart
Pork kidneys
Pork knuckle
Pork Lard
Pork liver
Pork lung
Pork marrow bones
Pork meat
Pork sausage (Bratwurst) Pork skin
Pork stomach
Pork/beef sausage (smoked)
Pork's intestine
Potato
Potato (mealy)

Potato flour
Prickly pear
Processed cheese 12%
processed cheese 30%
Psyllium seed
Pudding powder vanilla
Puff pastry
Pumpernickel (dark bread)
Pumpkin
Pumpkin seed oil
Pumpkin seeds
Quail
Quail egg
Quince
Quinoa
Rabbit
Rabbit (wild)
Rabbit liver
Rabbit meat
Radicchio
Radish
Radish (white, green, purple-red)
Radish black
Radish horseradish
Radish leaves
Raisins
Rapeseed oil
Raspberry
Raspberry dried (immature)
Raspberry jam
Raspberry leaf tea
Red beet
Red berry (without sugar)
Red cabbage
Red wine
Reishi mushroom
Rhubarb
Ribworttea
Rice (fragrance)
Rice (Gaoliang / Sorghum)
Rice (whole grain)
Rice Basmati
Rice black
Rice flour
Rice long grain rice
Rice malt
Rice mash
Rice noodles
Rice red
Rice round grain
Rice starch
Rice sticky
Rice sweet
Rice variety any

Rice wild (nature rice)
Romaine lettuce / lettuce salad
Rose blossom tea
Rose hip
Rose hip tea
Rose leaf tea
Rosefish
Rosemary
Rucola
Rusk
Rye
Rye flour
Rye wholemeal bread
Safflower (Dyer's thistle / Hong Hua)
Saffron
Sage
Sago (cereals)
Sake
Salmon
Salsify
Sauerkraut (cutted cabbage fermented)
Savory
Savoy cabbage / kale
Sea buckthorn
Sea cucumber
Seacrab
Sesame oil
Sesame oil roasted
Sesame paste (Tahini)
Sesame, black
Sesame, white
Shark
Sheep's milk
Sheep's milk yoghurt
Shiitake, dried
Shrimp
Shrimps
Skim milk powder
Slug
Sorrel
Sour cherries
Sour milk cheese 20%
Sourdough
Soy flour
Soy noodles
Soy sauce
Soy Tofu
Soy Tofu smoked
Soya Cuisine (soy cream)
Soybean milk
Soybean oil
Soybeans
Soybeans, black
Soybeans, blacks, fermented

Soybeans, yellow
Spelled (Dark) bread
Spelled flakes
Spelled grain
Spelled semolina
Spelled wholemeal flour
Spinach
Spiny lobsters
Spurdog (spiny dogfish, Schillerlocken)
St. Benedict's thistle, blessed thistle,
holy thistle, spotted thistle
Star anise
Stevia (candyleaf, sweetleaf)
Strawberries
Strawberry jam
Strawberry Juice
Sugar fructose - fruit sugar
Sugar glucose - grapes sugar
Sugar Milk Sugar
Sugar substitute (sweetener)
Sunflower oil
Sunflower seeds
Sweet potato
Tabasco
Tangerine
Tarragon (Estragon)
Tea mixture uric acid lowering
Thistle oil
Thyme
Thyme dried
Toast bread (whole grain)
Tomato
Tomato dried
Tomato juice
Tomato paste
Tomato puree
Tonic Water
Topinambur
Trout
Trout (smoked)
Truffle
Tsampa (roasted barley flour)
Tuna
Turkey breast meat
Turkey ham
Turmeric (yellow root)
Turnip
Turnips
Umeboshi paste
Umeboshi plums (Japanese apricots)
Valerian
Vanilla
Vanilla pod
Vanilla powder

Vanilla sugar natural
Vegetable juice
Vinegar (Apple vinegar)
Vinegar (Red wine vinegar)
Vinegar Aceto Balsamico
Vinegar Aceto Balsamico white
Wakame
Walnut oil
Water
Water hot
Watermelon
Wax gourd
Wheat
Wheat bran
Wheat bulgur
Wheat flakes
Wheat flatbread/pita bread
Wheat flour
Wheat flour whole grain
Wheat germ oil
Wheat semolina
Wheat semolina for children
Wheat/Rye/Gray-black bread with yeast
Wheatgrass juice
Wheatgrass powder
Whey

White beans
White bread (baguette)
White bread (pretzel sticks)
White bread (roll)
White bread (wheat bread)
White breadcrumbs
White cabbage
White dumpling bread (wheat bread cut into chunks)
Whitefish
Whole grain bread
Wholemeal flour
Wild boar meat
Wild garlic (garlic spinach)
Wild herbs
Wild strawberries
Wormwood herb
Yam root, yam root tuber
Yarrow
Yarrow tea
Yeast
Yew nut
Yoghurt vanilla
Yogi tea
Yogurt (natural, 1.5% fat)
Zucchini

10.3 Use ingredients: little

Beer (Pils)
Beer (Top-fermented German dark beer)
Bitter liqueur
Brown ale
Campari
Cola drink (low calorie)
Eel smoked
Fernet Branca (herbal bitter liqueur)
Ginseng liqueur
Honey wine (Met)
Lychee liqueur

Martini
Pineapple (from a can)
Prosecco
Rum
Salt
Salt (herbal)
Sherry (whine)
Spirit
Wheat beer
White wine
Wormwood

10.4 Do not use contra-acting foods

-

11 Herbs and their effects

11.1 Basil

It has a beneficial effect on flatulence and nausea, relaxing and soothing. Good to fight emphysema, bronchitis, whooping cough, high blood pressure, headache, mouth odor, warts, hiccup, gout, migraine.

11.2 Dill

The medicinal and spice herb has an antispasmodic effect and stimulates gastric juice production. Good to fight flatulence. Antispasmodic for gastrointestinal discomfort.

11.3 Coriander

The essential oils are appetizing, digestive, cramping and soothing in stomach and intestinal disorders.

11.4 Herbs various

Appetizing, lots of trace elements and vitamins

11.5 Cress

Diuretic, supports urination. Good to fight dry mouth, inner agitation, sore throat, diabetes, kidney stones, gastrointestinal complaints, lung problems, menstrual cramps or cancer.

11.6 Chives

Bactericide, prevents cancer, strengthens gastric juice production, promotes digestion and blood circulation, promotes growth, triggers stagnation.

11.7 Lovage

Stimulates digestion, reduces pain. Extracts of the root are used to flush out urinary tract infections and prevent kidney gravel.

11.8 Dandelion (young plants)

Detoxifies, relieves inflammation. Regulates digestion, helps with rheumatism, releases kidney stones, leaves pimples and chronic skin disorders disappear.

11.9 Oregano fresh

It has an anti-digestive, calming and nerve-strengthening effect, helps to fight cramping stomach and intestinal disorders. The ingredient Carvacrol has an anti-inflammatory effect.

11.10 Parsley

Stimulates liver function, detoxifies. Forces urinating. Relieves flatulence. Digestive and menstrual stimulating, birth-accelerating, memory-enhancing, blood-purifying, skin-smoothing.

11.11 Peppermint

Relaxes, frees the lungs and the nose (inhale), regulates the cycle. Stimulates bile flow and bile production, antispasmodic in gastrointestinal disorders, antimicrobial and antiviral.

11.12 Rosemary

Promotes digestion, relieves bloating, strengthens lung, spleen and kidney. Affects the circulation and nerves. Appetizing. Baths help to fight circulatory disorders as well as with gout and rheumatism.

11.13 Sage

Good to fight yeast infections. The leaves have a digestive effect and are used in greasy foods. Antiperspirant effect. Helps to relieve coughing attacks. Dries out (TCM).

11.14 Sorrel

Astringent, hematopoietic, purifies the blood, diuretic. Good to fight liver weakness, upset stomach, indigestion, constipation, diarrhea, worms, scurvy, anemia, women's complaints, wounds, skin rashes, boils, ulcers, swelling.

11.15 Black caraway

Detoxifying, immunoregulatory. In addition, the oil should stimulate the formation of bone marrow cells and generally protect body cells from viruses.

11.16   Thyme dried

Disinfecting. It stimulates the blood circulation, increases the appetite and helps to digest fat meat better. Strengthens lungs and spleen (TCM).

11.17   Lemongrass

Reduction of flatulence, antimicrobial, appetizing. Prevention of influenza. Good to fight infections in the mouth and throat.

12 Basics of Nutrition

The basic principles of nutrition described herein are general recommendations. They are not aimed at a specific form of therapy. Recommendations concerning a therapy have priority.

12.1 Nutrition

Regular meals in a relaxed atmosphere. A warm breakfast is considered a good start into the day.
The main meals ought to be taken for lunch – supper in the early evening. Pay attention to feeling hungry or sated: don't eat too much nor remain hungry is the rule
Prepare the meals freshly from natural, regional products. Frozen, heat-conserved, industrially prepared or foodstuffs cooked in the microwave oven are rejected.
Choice of foodstuffs according to the season: more cooling food in summer, more warming food in winter.
Eat cooked food at least twice a day. Food and drinks ought to be lukewarm, never ice-cold or hot.
Raw vegetables, briefly cooked vegetables, freshly squeezed juices and mineral water are not recommended. Milk and dairy products are only included in the diet if they don't cause problems.
Don't use therapeutic recipes over a longer period without consulting your doctor or therapist.

Varied food
Enjoy the diversity of foodstuffs. Characteristics of a balanced nutrition are variety, suitable combination and a balanced quantity of rich and low energy foodstuffs (on one hand avoiding undersupply with essential nutrients and on the other hand to take to many undesirable substances).

A lot of Cereal Products - and Potatoes
Bread, pasta, rice, cereal flakes (best wholemeal) as well as potatoes contain almost no fat, but many vitamins, mineral nutrients, trace elements, roughage and secondary plant substances. These foodstuffs ought to be taken with low-fat side dishes.

Vegetables and Fruit – „Take Five" every day …
5 portions of vegetables and fruit a day, as fresh as possible, briefly cooked, or maybe one portion as a juice – ideal as a side dish to every meal as well as snack between meals: Thus a lot of vitamins, mineral nutrients as well as roughage and secondary plant substances

Daily milk and dairy products
Milk and Dairy Products every Day, once or twice per Week Fish;
meat, sausages as well as eggs moderately. These foodstuffs contain
valuable nutrients like calcium in the milk, iodine selenium and omega-3
fat acids in saltwater fish. Meat is favorable due to its high content of
disposable iron and the vitamins B1, B6 and B12. Quantities of 300 – 600
g meat and sausage per week are sufficient. Prefer low-fat products,
especially in meat- and dairy products.

Low-fat and fatty Foodstuffs
Fat supplies us with essential fat acids and fatty foodstuffs contain also
fat-soluble vitamins. Fat is high in energy; therefore much fat in the food
may cause overweight, possibly also cancer. Too many saturated fat
acids may further a tendency for cardio-vascular diseases in the long
term. Prefer vegetable oils and fats (e.g. rapeseed-, olive-, soya-oils and
solid fats produced therefrom). Beware of invisible fat in meat- and dairy
products, pastry and sweets as well as in fast-food and convenience
foods. 70 – 90 g fat per day is sufficient.

Moderately Sugar and Salt
Take sugar and foods/drinks containing various kinds of sugar (e.g.
glucose syrup) only occasionally. Use herbs and spices as well as a little
salt creatively. Prefer salt containing iodine.

Plenty of Liquids
Water is absolutely essential. Drink 1-2 l liquids every day. Prefer water
(with or without gas) and other low-calorie drinks. Alcoholic drinks should
not be taken.

Tasty Dishes, carefully cooked
Cook the meals with as low temperatures and as short as possible, using
little water and fat – this preserves the original taste, keeps the nutrients
intact and prevents the production of harmful compounds.

Take time and enjoy the food
Take your Time and enjoy your Food
Eating consciously helps to eat right. The eye enjoys food, too. It's fun,
invites to enjoy varied dishes and stimulates the feeling of satiety.

Watch your Weight and stay in Motion
A balanced diet and a lot of exercise and sport (30 – 60 min/day) are a
healthy combination. The right weight furthers well-being and health.
Thermals, directional effectiveness, digestive power

There are various criteria for judging the effectiveness of herbs and foodstuffs.

The use of certain herbs and ingredients is based on observations of the effects on the body which these foodstuffs, herbs and spices show after having eaten them. The medical science has developed following system: Every ingredient or herb has a directional effectiveness. Furthermore, there are herbs which have a special effect on certain organs.

The basic condition for a healthy metabolism is to obtain sufficient energy from food and that the digestive process doesn't use too much energy. An easily digestible meal makes content and sated, doesn't cause flatulence and fatigue after the meal. The perfect spices increase the healthiness of our meals. Very often, just small doses of herbs and spices will suffice. They are not used to make us sated, but to help our digestive organs to digest the food.

12.2 Recipes

The recipes list the ingredients to be used and the cooking instructions show how the dish is prepared. The list of ingredients shows the concerned quantities as well as the relevance for the therapy. If you find „less than mentioned", try to comply or find an alternative from the „list of recommended foodstuffs". Mostly it shall result just in a small change of taste when you simply avoid this ingredient.

Mild cooking methods: boiling, stewing, poaching, steaming
Strong cooking methods: barbecuing, roasting, frying, smoking
Balanced cooking methods: deep-frying, baking brick
Deep-freezing and warming in the microwave oven should be avoided (denaturalization).

12.3 Foodstuffs

Foodstuffs have an effect on body and soul like medicinal herbs, only a very much milder one. Dietary advice is mainly based on regional foodstuffs. The knowledge about the effects of each foodstuff and the knowledge, when which foodstuff shall be used, is based on the orthodoschool of medicine. Use ecologic-organic products, if possible. As everything should be cooked for a long time due to a better digestability and very rarely eaten raw, the food agrees with everyone.

The classification of the foodstuffs according to their effect on the body is the basis in order to achieve a harmonious status of health.

Dietary advisors do not recommend certain foodstuffs for everyone. The individual diet is tailor-made for the individual constitution.

Buy only fresh and ripe fruit and vegetables. You ought to leave unripe fruit and vegetables and such with brown spots and wilted leaves behind in the market. In this case take deep-frozen goods (never ready-to-serve dishes!). Fruit and vegetables are deep-frozen immediately after harvesting and often contain more vitamins and minerals than the goods from the vegetable shelf. Whereas conserved or tinned goods contain very much less biological substances. Also, salt, sugar and others are mostly added to the latter. Never leave the foodstuffs in the water after washing them to avoid that many vital substances get drowned. Clean salads, fruit and vegetables immediately before serving.

Please make sure of the hygienic processing of foodstuffs. Clean your salads, fruit and vegetables carefully. When cooking with meat, prepare all ingredients first and then process the meat products. Clean the worktop and tools very carefully. Wooden surfaces ought to be treated with a mild disinfectant regularly in order to reduce germination.

Store fruit and vegetables separately, if possible. Harvested fruit and vegetables are still alive and emit e.g. ethylene gas, which makes other products ripen and age faster. Keep meat and fish in the closed packaging or store them in the fridge in closed containers.

12.4 Herbs

There are some basic rules for storing medicinal herbs. On principle, herbs must be protected from direct sunlight, humidity and heat.

Containers for the storage of herbs may be glasses, ceramic jars and even plastic containers. However, plastic is a rather unsuitable material and should only be a short-term solution. In case of glass containers, use a dark material.

Medicinal herbs cannot be kept for any long period. The shelf life of herbs is limited. However, it can be prolonged with suitable storage. The place should be dark, rather cool and absolutely dry. A wooden medicine cabinet, placed not directly next to a source of heat, would be ideal. Never buy large quantities of herbs so as not to have to throw them away. Label the container with the name of the herb and the date of harvesting or processing.

13 Other dietic-books

The following syndromes of dietetics, TCM or for a therapy supplement for cancer are available.

Dietetics

E001. Nutrition of the infant - baby food
E002. Nutrition during lactation
E003. Nutrition in old age
E004. Nutrition of children and adolescents
E005. Nutrition of athletes
E006. Light weight
E007. Pregnancy
E008. Full food

Protein and electrolyte - kidneys
E009. (hemodialysis) dialysis treatment
E010. Acute renal failure
E011. Chronic renal insufficiency
E012. Nephrotic syndrome
E013. Kidney stones (nephrolithiasis)

Gastrointestinal tract - pancreas
E014. Acute pancreatitis (inflammation of the pancreas)
E015. Chronic pancreatitis (inflammation of the pancreas)

Gastrointestinal tract - small intestine and large intestine
E016. Acute obstipation (constipation)
E017. Chronic obstipation (constipation)
E018. Colon irritabile
E019. Diverticulitis
E020. Acquired lactose intolerance (lactose malabsorption)
E021. Fructose malabsorption
E022. Glutensensitive enteropathy (celiac disease)
E023. Colectomy
E024. Short Bowel Syndrome

Gastrointestinal tract - liver, gallbladder, bile ducts
E025. Acute and chronic hepatitis (inflammation of the liver)
E026. Cholelithiasis (bile stones)
E027. fatty liver
E028. cirrhosis

Gastrointestinal tract - Stomach and duodenal intestine
E029. Acute gastritis
E030. Chronic gastritis
E031. Stomach bleeding
E032. Ulcus ventriculi and duodenal ulcer
E033. Condition after gastric surgery

Gastrointestinal tract - oral cavity and esophagus
E034. Stomatitis
E035. Esophageal carcinoma (esophageal cancer)
E036. Refluosophagitis (heartburn)

Special diseases
E037. Phenylketonuria (PKU)
E038. Rheumatic joint diseases

Metabolism
E039. Obesity (overweight)
E040. Diabetes mellitus
E041. Eating disorders (underweight)

Fat metabolism
E042. Hypercholesterolaemia (increased cholesterol level)
E043. Hepatic Encephalopathy

Heart and circulation
E044. Arteriosclerosis (arterial calcification)
E045. Heart insufficiency
E046. Hypertension
E047. Hyperuricaemia and gout

Changed nutrient requirements
E048. In case of fever
E049. For malignant diseases
E050. After burns
E051. Radiation and chemotherapy

CANCER
E100. Pancreatic cancer
E101. Bladder cancer
E102. Blood cancer (leukemia)
E103. Breast cancer
E104. Colorectal cancer
E105. Gastric cancer
E106. Kidney cancer
E107. Esophageal cancer

TCM
E200. Bladder - moisture heat in the bladder
E201. Bladder - moisture and cold in the bladder
E202. Bladder - emptiness and cold in the bladder
E203. Large intestine - external cold affects the large intestine
E204. Large intestine - moisture heat in the large intestine
E205. Large intestine - heat blocks the intestine II acute
E206. Large intestine - dryness of the colon
E207. Large intestine - Yang deficiency (cold)
E208. Heart - Blood insufficiency
E209. Heart - Blood stagnation
E210. Heart - Fire
E211. Heart - Hot mucus clogs the heart pores

E212. Heart - Cold mucus clogs the heart pores
E213. Heart - Qi deficiency
E214. Heart - Yang deficiency
E215. Heart - Yin deficiency
E216. Liver - Ascending Liver Yang
E217. Liver - Blood deficiency
E218. Liver - Blood stagnation
E219. Liver - Moisture heat in liver and gall bladder
E220. Liver - Fire
E221. Liver - Gall bladder Qi-Empty
E222. Liver - Cold in the liver meridian
E223. Liver - Qi stagnation
E224. Liver - Wind
E225. Liver - Wind with ascending liver Yang
E226. Liver - Wind with blood anemic
E227. Liver - Wind with extreme heat
E228. Lung - Qi deficiency
E229. Lung - Mucus-moisture in the lungs
E230. Lung - Mucus-heat in the lungs
E231. Lung - Mucus-cold in the lungs
E232. Lung - Dryness of the lungs
E233. Lung - Wind-heat attacks the lungs
E234. Lung - Wind-cold affects the lungs
E235. Lung - Yin deficiency
E236. Stomach - Bloodstagnation
E237. Stomach - Fire
E238. Stomach - Cold with liquid
E239. Stomach - Nutrition stagnation
E240. Stomach - Qi deficiency
E241. Stomach - Rebellious Qi
E242. Stomach - Yin Emptiness
E243. Spleen - Heat and moisture attack the spleen
E244. Spleen - Coldness and moisture affects the spleen
E245. Spleen - Qi deficiency
E246. Spleen - Qi deficiency + Declining spleen Qi
E247. Spleen - Qi deficiency + spleen does not control the blood
E248. Spleen - Yang deficiency
E249. Kidney - Heart and kidney no longer communicate
E250. Kidney - Jing deficiency
E251. Kidney - Kidneys cannot receive the Qi
E252. Kidney - Qi is not stable
E253. Kidney - Yang deficiency
E254. Kidney - Yin deficiency

For further information visit di-book.com.